STAB🗡TAGE!

How to Deal with the Pit Bulls, Skunks, Snakes, Scorpions & Slugs in the Health Care Workplace

Dr. Judith Briles

Author of *Zapping Conflict in the Health Care Workplace*

**mile high
press**

www.MileHighPress.com

Books may be purchased for sales promotion
by contacting the publisher,
Mile High Press at PO Box 460880 Aurora CO 80046
303-627-9179 ~ 303-627-9184 Fax ~ MileHighPress@aol.com

Library of Congress Catalog # 2008927105

ISBN: 978-1-885331-30-4

1. Business   2. Management   3. Health   4. Nursing

First Edition   Printed in Canada

For Diann and Jo ...

Visionary women who see, feel, think and care.

Table of Contents

1

Are There Staboteurs™ in Your (Workplace) Midst? In a Nutshell, **Yes**

... My health
deteriorated to the point I
was seeing pain specialists because I was
having serious physical side effects.
Survey Respondent #14

I magine yourself faced with a problem that won't go away. A problem that didn't even have a name until just a few years ago. The problem keeps growing, threatening to destroy your workplace. If not resolved, you may lose your job, or key individuals will quit, or the word will spread that no one who is in her right mind wants to work with your team.

The problem mushrooms. In your most recent evaluation, you are criticized for not dealing with the hostility and tension in your group. Everything that you learned in your post-degree classes seems for naught—nothing ever addressed the issues you are experiencing in the types of covert activities when women work with other women. Your self-doubts are building; you begin to feel paranoid. Is someone trying to cut your job out from under you?

One day, after a series of events, you do lose your coveted job. The woman you had mentored the past year had given incorrect information to your manager. Folders and files have mysteriously disappeared from your computer. What you thought was a perfect workplace life is not so perfect. In fact, it's a mess.

You are now plagued by recurring nightmares, nightmares that are so horrible that you don't want to remember anything about them in the morning. When you wake, you feel as though you are choking to death. You've concluded that the business world is the pits and wonder why you ever left your first love of teaching history.

You feel like an emotional and physical wreck. You seek professional help, yet nothing works. Your friends are worried. So are you.

You are not alone. Others echo your experiences. Both your sisters work in health care. One's an administrator in a hospital in the South, the other is a critical care nurse in a large hospital in the city where you live and work. Each has reported the same phenomenon in their workplace. When you hear them say, "Nurses eat their young," you tell them, "It's not just nurses, it's women in general who eat their young. If I had my druthers, I would rather work with men."

I used to call this phenomenon *sabotage*—this was a problem among women in the workplace first identified in my book, *Woman to Woman: From Sabotage to Support* in 1987. Now I call it "stabotage™." It's much worse.

How naïve I was 20 plus years ago to think that all I had to do to fix this mess was to report that women were undermining each other in the workplace, supply the study to support the research data and write and publish the first book on the topic. Woven with painful and telling stories, it ended with a laundry list of solutions.

My expectation was that women would read it, talk about it and implement my recommendations ... and viola, they would stop undermining each other.

Fast-forward to this century. With nine studies and six additional books later covering the topic (*GenderTraps, Woman to Woman 2000, The SeXX Factor* (co-written with Mary Lou Ryder),*The Briles Report on Women in Health Care, Zapping Conflict in the Health Care Workplace* and now *Stabotage!*), the storyline continues. Books have also been written by others and added to the dialogue; they are mostly anecdotal.

Unfortunately, sabotage in the workplace is alive and well. The results of the current study are not good. In a nutshell, women (and men) are still undermining each other, and in many ways; we are doing it so much better with the communication capabilities we have available today.

It's now time to add a new word to our lexicon: stabotage. There's a fine line between sabotage and stabotage, but it's an important one....

> *Stabotage* **is the mayhem, destruction, backstabbing, frontstabbing, betrayal, treachery, seduction and damage that women (and men) encounter in their personal and professional lives that are *intentionally* generated by another. It leads to loss of credibility, confidence and reputation with yourself as well as with others. In contrast, *sabotage* can be unintentional, as well as intentional.**

Once again, it's time to put on my researcher and interviewer hats and head back to the writing desk.

You'll learn what's new (and old) in the wide world of undermining and betrayal, learn to weigh out the damage that the *staboteur*™ does, and come away with practical tools that you can use to deal with these destructive forces—the Pit Bulls, Skunks, Snakes, Scorpions and Slugs in your workplace.

2

The Survey Speaks ...
Stabotage in
Your Workplace

I felt so unsafe and have not
gone back to work for fear of it
happening again. I know that patients
are now suffering because I am
no longer at the abusing facility.
Survey Respondent #337

Since the first book that focused on undermining, conflict and sabotaging activities was published in 1987, I've criss-crossed several continents speaking on the topic ... and listening to women and men talk about their workplaces. I've heard the good, the bad and the ugly ... the very good and the very ugly.

Truth be told, comments about the ugly outweighed the good too many times. Naively, by bringing attention to the issue, offering methods to deal with it, I kept thinking that it would correct itself and go away. Wrong.

Today, conflict is very much alive and, unfortunately, doing quite well in its expansion activities. In some workplaces, it's actually enabled by the benign neglect of management. Most say,

> Yes, we know there is bad behavior and conflict at work.

Simple enough. I then ask,

> What steps are you taking to reduce and eliminate rotten behavior and conflict?
>
> Are you tuned in to the true cost of the reduced productivity and morale that the bad behavior creates?
>
> How about the exit factor—what does it really cost to replace a good employee when she or he finally says, "Screw it, I'm out of here," and seeks employment elsewhere?

The response ... Silence. Stammering. "I'll get back to you." Etc., Etc., Etc.

The Health Care Workplace Needs a Doctor

The new study results for this latest book again showed that all is not well. Still. This time, focusing on sabotage, some of the questions I asked included—

- Is there sabotage in your workplace?
- In what form have you observed or experienced it?
- Has sabotage increased, decreased or not changed in the past five years?
- What do you think the reasons for the change (if any) are?

- Do you have a preference for working with men or women?
- Do the generations display sabotaging behavior differently? How?
- How do your manager or co-workers handle it when it occurs?
- How do you react when you observe sabotaging behavior?
- What do you do when it happens to you?
- What has been the cost/effect to you?
- If you had the power, what would you do to the sabotage creator?

The study results and interviews that followed birthed the new word, "stabotage."

Conflict is when two or more people assume opposing and different positions in a situation or circumstance.

Sabotage is the *intentional or unintentional* undermining or destruction of another's personal or professional integrity.

Stabotage is the *intentional* undermining or destruction of another's personal or professional integrity.

Conflict, Sabotage and *Stabotage* can be expressed verbally or nonverbally and presented in an overt or covert method. If not acknowledged, dealt with and resolved in a timely manner, morale dives, loyalty diminishes, teams are splintered, distrust grows and turnover increases.

Ongoing conflict, sabotage and stabotage costs an organization multimillions of dollars a year in lost productivity, search fees and training costs for replacement of personnel.

As previous surveys (eight) have shown, when it comes to conflict, sabotage and stabotaging behaviors, men do not discriminate: they behave unprofessionally toward both genders. Their style of creating conflict and undermining activities still shows a variance from women's: men are more overt and more direct when they are underminers. Interestingly, many of the respondents reported that they saw it coming.

Women still showed the tendency to be less direct, choosing the covert method of displaying negative behavior toward another. And, when a woman was an underminer, her target would most likely be another woman. Respondents here reported that sometimes they literally didn't know what hit them; they didn't see it coming.

Negative behaviors that are not honestly addressed mean the difference between black and red on a financial statement. Not addressing conflict and allowing it and any form of sabotage to continue are the leading causes for why good people exit a workplace and mediocre ones are enabled to breed.

It means the difference between having moneys to continue your activities, enhance the work environment, educate staff and hire the best talent—or being in the red. Red means disaster—moneys are drained, employee satisfaction plummets, staff and management exits for greener pastures, errors multiply and patients are put at risk because the "talent" that is left behind to care for them isn't so talented.

Who's Who ... The Survey and Respondents

A 74-question survey was initially distributed via the Internet, with the first wave directly from the *Briles.com* website through a link directly to a nonpartisan group that specializes in gathering data. Answers to the questions were either a Yes, No, Not Sure, Multiple Choice or Open-ended, which required a written response.

All respondents were anonymous. After the initial distribution to approximately 1,800 potential respondents, the link was redistributed randomly by the original takers to others.

Each questionnaire was accompanied by a cover letter, which identified the purpose of the survey, including the promise that the results would be released in a future book. Respondents were also given the option of participating in an interview at a later date. When they did, they chose to reveal their names and contact information.

The 2008 survey respondents came solely from a variety of health care related companies and organizations over a three-month period. More than 3,000 respondents (actual number at cutoff was 3,217)—nurses, doctors, dentists, hygienists, administrators, directors of various departments, vice presidents of nursing, staff of educational departments, employees of pharmaceutical and other health-related organizations.

Who was who in our survey? Seven percent were male and 93 percent female ... not surprising for a health care sampling. Of the entire total, 46 percent identified themselves as employees-staff and 54 percent management-administration.

When asked how many years they had worked in health care, more than 41 percent reported 20 years or more, 22 percent stated 11 to 19 years, and 27 percent responded less than 10 years.

Key Findings

The lead questions were: *Is there sabotaging or abusive/ bullying behavior in your current workplace? Have you ever* left a job because of abusive or bullying behavior created by another? and Has sabotage or abusive/bullying behavior increased, decreased or not changed in the past five years?

Is there sabotaging, abusive or bullying behavior in your current workplace?

Yes	55%
No	34%
Not sure	11%

Have you ever left a job because of abusive or bullying behavior created by another?

Yes	51%
No	48%
Not sure	1%

Has sabotage or abusive/bullying behavior increased, decreased or not changed in the past five years?

Increased	56%
Decreased	25%
Not Sure	19%

Accountability was critical in dealing with bad behavior. Those who reported a decrease added that some form of code of conduct was instituted around accountability and correction. If the behavior persisted, termination. Comments were made about management participating in crucial conversation classes and the positive effect they had, and the integrity of upper management in not allowing bad behavior.

Some of the reasons cited for increased bad behavior included: "good old girls club," it's just tolerated, old habits are hard to break, too much change, competition, scrambling for survival, the union, lesser paid and inexperienced people, cultures that reward aggressive behavior to generate short-term results at any cost, people don't confront, and, they can get away with it.

Who created it? (more than one answer could be marked)

Manager	63%
Co-worker	36%
Patient/Family Member	3%
Physician	2%

What was the gender of the abuser/bully?

Male	26%
Female	58%
Both	16%

What type of behavior was displayed? (This was an open-ended question; responses were one word to two pages—below is a summary without percentages—no single type is identified; all reflect multiple replies from all respondents.)

Gossip, lying, bullying, degrading, serial targeting, fired without warning, belittling, screaming, false accusations, name calling, intimidation, physical threats, sexual harassment, abusive language, behind my back bullying, setting up roadblocks, grabbing arms and shaking, undermining decisions in front of others, withholding information and not communicating, taking another's credit, sneaking behind others' backs, rudeness, yelling, throwing things, stalking, favoritism, lack of respect, character defamation, told to lie, slander, and accusations of stealing money.

Some of the stories shared by the respondents have been included in *Stabotage!* Hundreds of the survey respondents took the time to write out detailed descriptions of what happened to them. One nurse wrote after sharing her saga: "I haven't practiced as an RN since December 2006. I'm afraid to work with women again. To this day, I can still feel every knife that was stuck in my back."

What did the abusive/bullying behavior cost you?
(multiple responses allowed)

Stress	90%
Loss of Confidence	47%
Productivity loss	46%
My job	45%
Loss of reputation	30%
Health	15%
Other	10%

"Other" included multiple write-in comments relating to: lost respect for others, lost respect for administration, becoming stubborn and vindictive, and allowing my "bad side" to surface.

What did the perpetrator gain? (multiple responses allowed)

Enhanced reputation	28%
Ego–Power	25%
Promotion	10%
My job	6%

Money	5%
Nothing	5%
Other	71%

On evaluation of "Other" revealed that the 45 percent who had lost their jobs had marked this option. The responses ranged from, "I left, I have no idea what she gained," to "She finally got fired" to "Payback ... she had a heart attack."

Would you return to the workplace if the abusive person no longer worked there?

Yes	29%
No	51%
Not sure	20%

Respondents who said "No" included a variety of reasons: Management allows it to continue; top management positions are seeded with similar persons; too embarrassed, I don't know what was said about me after I left; the overall culture hasn't changed; the entire place is evil; just too negative; other people were poisoned against me; too much politics; no one could print enough money to get me to return to that place; I'm now working for myself; and I moved on and UP.

Do you ever have to "cover" for someone in your workplace because of their incompetence?

Yes	52%
No	48%
Not sure	0%

When asked the position of the person they covered, 36 percent of the respondents said it was for someone higher than their position.

If you had a magic wand, what would you like management to do about this person(s)?

Terminate	45%
Warn	18%
Suspend	4%
Move somewhere else	2%
Other	31%

Depending on what the "incompetency" was, responses under the "Other" option were broad. The great majority wrote that extensive counseling and/or training should be required and, if not successful, then termination, just get her away from me, it's moot, and jail would be too good.

If you are a woman, do you prefer to work with men, women, or does it matter?

Women	4%
Men	26%
Either	70%

If you are a man, do you prefer to work with men, women, or does it matter?

Women	19%
Men	4%
Either	77%

The reponses to these two questions are a mixed bag. The great news is that for the first time in 20 years there is a decline in the percentage of women reporting that they prefer *not* to work with other women. Previous studies have reported approximately one-third of women prefer working with men. The Stabotage study found a reduction of 26 percent.

In a female-dominated workplace, where 26 percent of the workforce shows a bias against the dominant gender, there will be significant problems. In health care, patient safety is at risk.

Do generations display sabotage or abusive/bullying behavior differently?

Yes	51%
No	16%
Not sure	33%

No one disputes that there are differences between the generations. Where the Gen Xers and Millennials are very outcome-oriented, Boomers are task-oriented. In the first decade of the 21st century, the Boomers represent the majority of a hospital workplace.

According to the survey, Gen Xers and Millennials don't understand why Boomers put energy into tasks where an outcome isn't created and measured—it's a waste of time for them. The oldest generation, the Matures, don't like conflict of any sort and would like it to just go away.

The survey shows that when it comes to an issue that is generated from any type of conflict, both Gen Xer's and Millennial's style is to jump in—decorum and diplomacy aren't their strengths.

How do your manager or co-workers handle sabotage, abusive/bullying behavior and conflict when it occurs? (multiple responses allowed)

Bury their head and hopes it goes away	38%
Deal with it immediately	33%
Put it off	20%
Contribute to it	19%
Other	14%

Most of the "Other" category would fit into burying, dealing with, putting it off, or contributing to it, when responses were analyzed. Some, though, said: tells everyone to get along; sends out memos telling us how ungrateful we are; ignores the basic problems; couldn't care less; talks about it, gossips about it, feeds on it; gives the other the benefit of the doubt; depends on who is doing it and how blatant it is; and, from one manager, "I don't put up with this crap."

How do you react when you observe sabotaging or abusive/bullying behavior? (multiple responses allowed)

Speak up against it	69%
Try to sidestep it	24%
Ignore it	6%
Participate in it	1%
Other	16%

The "Others" added to their comments. One wrote: "It depends. At times I speak up if I feel I can make a difference." Another wrote: "Different levels require different reactions—sometimes the subtle abuse that occurs everyday isn't recognized immediately as abuse." And another: "I want to speak up, but I become fearful of retribution."

What do you do when it happens to you? (multiple responses allowed)

Confront it	70%
Hope that someone intervenes	15%
Ignore it	13%
Deny that it happened	1%
Other	17%

Many of the "Others" added to their comments in this question also. Comments like: "I tried to ignore it, but it backfired." "I wanted to go to HR, but I didn't want to be labeled as a trouble-maker." "Unfortunately, I wear my feelings on my sleeve and my emotions take over..." "I get upset, but can't report it ... no one wants to listen and the 'bullier' is in management." "I plan a subtle retaliation for later." "If it's someone I feel I can deal with, I do. If it's management, I leave it alone. I'm in the process of bully-proofing myself and helping others to do the same." And, "I've learned to pick my battles."

One of the respondents even offered a definition of a 'bullier' ... an experienced, tenured bully.

When management doesn't deal with sabotaging, abusive or bullying behavior, how do you react? (multiple responses allowed)

I lose respect for the organization	64%
I lose respect for my managers	62%
I think about looking for another job	50%
My loyalty is reduced	49%
I do everything to avoid the person	48%
My productivity declines	36%
I feel my workplace is the pits	32%
Other	11%

In reviewing the "Others" additional comments, they basically supported most of the responses that could be marked, then added to them. One wrote, "I become discouraged and withdraw and don't want to have anything do with that person; I warn others." Many added comments like, "If it's me, I'm out of there. If it's someone else, I advise them to leave the job, especially if the abuser is the boss or her relative, or has a physical relationship with the boss."

Several nurses pointed out that patient care suffers: "As a nurse, if my patient is being cared for by an abusive doctor, I will be less likely to call him with concerns or observations. I will second guess myself more often. Just placing a call is traumatic because I know in advance that I will be verbally abused."

Money Always Talks ...Does Anyone Listen?

In my consulting, sometimes I work with a solo hospital, sometimes with an entire system, and sometimes with the mother ship—the overseer of the system. With one mother ship, I was appalled at the level of duplicity among several of the staff, right under the noses of the senior administrators.

The reported actions of the staff members toward others within the staff didn't surprise me nor did the overall inattentiveness to the problem from their bosses, HR and administrators—nothing was really new. I'd heard about it, seen it and experienced it repeatedly since I had focused on the health care workplace in the early nineties.

After multiple interviews and training sessions, I wrote a detailed report and made recommendations on how to deal with the women who were the primary creators of the conflicting behaviors among the 40 women who worked there. The administrators were told that if they didn't deal with it fairly quickly, they would lose several key employees.

What did they do with what I gave them? *Nothing, absolutely nothing.* Within their office, several key employees tossed in the towel and said, "I've had it . . . enough is enough," and sought work elsewhere. When will management learn and get its act together?

The financial costs are unbelievable, ranging from lost productivity to placement fees for new personnel. Replacement experts and health care organizations report that replacing an employee, especially in a "shortage" environment, can range anywhere from 100 to 300 percent of the annual income of an employee. Even a small facility can spend in hard and soft dollars millions in replacement-related costs. A large percentage of that can be attributed directly to conflict, sabotage and stabotage. Big, big bucks.

Organizations are collectively losing billions of dollars a year due to lost productivity. Stabotage, sabotage and conflict in the workplace isn't a lightweight issue, nor should it be treated as one. Unfortunately, it is. Everyday, hospitals keep their Losers and lose their Keepers.

Summing Up

Stabotage, sabotage and conflict are alive and all too well in health care. The cost to any department and organization is significant in human and financial costs. And, it's increasing yearly.

Health care is one of the few industries that shows growth across the board (yet also significant financial losses in unreimbursed expenses). Many health care positions are routinely placed in the "most secure" job category to have in national surveys.

The good news is that great and good people can leave an unhealthy workplace. It's also the bad news. It means that mediocre staff and management stay behind. Most sick environments don't want to take their own pulse and temp to see how they are doing; they are blinded to many of the behavior problems that create toxic workplaces.

When action is taken to alter a negative workplace, morale, loyalty and productivity increase; teams are strengthened; stress levels are reduced; turn-over decreases; management is viewed as proactive; and money is saved.

The chapters that follow focus on who, what and how toxic people—the pit bulls, skunks, snakes, scorpions and slugs—got there and how to deal with them. The newly revised *CarefrontingScript*™ introduced in Chapter 9 will empower those that use it and de-power those that create the need for it.

3

Identifying Pit Bulls, Skunks, Snakes, Scorpions & Slugs in the Workplace

F ew will admit to being a staboteur. After all, stabotage is an intentional and blatant slamming of another, not something that could have been misconstrued or unintentional. When a staboteur is a Pit Bull, for example, it's obvious who the culprit is.

Pit Bulls may even tell you ahead of time that you are the game. Their positioning could be, "Tomorrow at 3 PM, I'm going to shred your credibility at the staff meeting." Part of their game plan is for you to be an active participant, to shake in your shoes a bit until the big unveiling of whatever the Pit Bull has planned.

Not so with the other staboteurs. Slugs and Skunks wouldn't think of being so bold if they were going to set another up; Snakes and Scorpions would admire the Pit Bull for her boldness, but would personally prefer the finesse of striking at another by a more covert method, and then act oblivious to the chaos that's created. A subtle backstab fits their MO.

Confronting staboteurs is essential in decreasing and eliminating their activity. If you don't know who's doing it, you can't confront and get closure. And, closure is important.

Unique Factors in the Health Care Workplace

The genders do display a difference in how they create and respond to sabotage and stabotage. Surveys that my company has coordinated for the past 20 plus years have repeatedly reported that men are more inclined to be overt if they are staboteurs; women are inclined to be covert.

The majority of the respondents have reported that men were non-discriminatory; they would undermine either gender while women were more inclined to target their own gender. If a man was a target, he was more inclined to confront the saboteur while a woman was less inclined to confront, but she would share what happened with others.

Although a significant percentage of men didn't report that they had a gender preference for whom they worked ... women did. Over one quarter of the female respondents stated that they didn't want to work with other women.

These unique factors can create a disruptive workplace. In the case of women not wanting to work with other women, patients can be at risk. If one nurse doesn't like another nurse and a call for assistance comes in, the other nurse may elect not to treat the request with any priority.

Pass the Cake

For co-workers, the fear of potential harm from a saboteur or staboteur to them personally or professionally creates an environment that is highly stressful and toxic. That means they are less productive, morale takes a dive, and common goals within the organization suffer. Key employees start looking for new jobs—the toxicity isn't worth it—no matter how much they get paid.

Whether you are a manager or an employee, ignorance isn't bliss. You've got to deal with sabotage and undermining activities in your workplace. If you don't, you can lose big—your reputation, your position, and your bottom line. Money.

When I interviewed Kim, I knew from her reputation that she was an accomplished MD in the field of orthopedic surgery. Prior to her MD, she was an OR nurse. Her story has been one of those that you don't forget.

Kim told me that she will never forget the going-away party given by her nursing colleagues as she began medical school. It wins my meanness award: a party to which everyone was invited except the honoree, Kim. She shared,

I was excluded. I wasn't even invited. I knew a party was going on.

I was still working in the operating room. They just didn't invite me!

Initially, I couldn't believe what I had heard Kim say. To my knowledge, this was a first. I have spoken to thousands of women and men over the years, hearing story after story. Some stories were so absurd I couldn't help laughing. Others communicated the teller's deep pain. Kim continued,

I had worked in the operating room for five years. On my last day of work, I was involved in a very intricate plastic-surgery case. Normally, my shift is over at three o'clock. At that time, I should have gone to the party. That's when it began. At least, that's what I was told later.

No one was sent in to tell me or relieve me, so I stayed and finished the case. It lasted until six o'clock that evening. On my way out of the operating room, I picked up my "surprise" going-away gift, a piece of cake, and a note that said, "Good luck" which were left for me on the desk. I was ready to begin a new life.

Kim never knew if there was one person who set up the mock party or if there were several players. The good news is that she didn't waste her time and energy in trying to track down the staboteur... and it *was* a stabotage, an intentional act of undermining.

Stabbing Staboteur

As the new director of Surgical Services in the Southwest, Abby had to learn to deal with her staff directly. Her own personal experience is that nursing is a profession in which we try to cover for others, letting them slip by on bad behavior because it is so difficult to have those "crucial conversations," not recognizing the harm and dysfunction we create by our lack of courage.

Abby had to terminate a long-time manager within her first week. The environment that had been created in this manager's department was riddled with fear and mistrust. Abby shared,

This manager was actually on vacation during my first week as the new director. I met with staff and reviewed prior documentation of multiple instances in which HR had historically needed to intervene in this department with complaints of harassment and other situations that indicated a lack of integrity. It became clear to me that operations in this key support department were completely dysfunctional due to the leadership style (or lack thereof) of this long-time manager. I felt we were at a crisis point that required immediate and decisive action. I discussed my assessment with HR and hospital senior leadership, and received complete support to move forward.

I had never even met this manager, but I called her while she was still on vacation and told her that from the assessment I had done and the review of the situation, I had no confidence in her ability to effectively lead the team in her department and told her that her employment was terminated, effective immediately.

Of course, I anticipated I would get the 'How could you do this?!' response that you usually get from staff or peers when action like this is taken, but it was unbelievably silent. In fact, you could almost hear an audible sigh of relief.

Since then, I have new leadership in this department, and the OR as well, and the entire team is thriving. Our latest employee satisfaction scores showed significant improvement since the pre-firing era. Even the surgeons make frequent comments to administration about the dramatic change in the entire surgical and perioperative departments.

Abby has learned her management and leadership skills through the school of hard knocks. Her experience

over the years has shown that some employees can suck
life out of people. Examples she gave included: not show-
ing up, manipulating circumstances, not doing the job, just
being negative, multiple clinical errors—just bringing the
team down. Abby continues,

> The bad ones croak very loud—like toads. One
> especially memorable nurse had worked in the
> same department for over 25 years. Bertha was
> known for her power plays and was literally
> physically intimidating; often, she would befriend
> anyone new, acting like she was their mentor. To
> her, knowledge was power.
>
> Once she had them indebted to her over a
> period of several months, she would then proceed
> to bad-mouth nursing administration, the unit
> leadership team, and even her peers. Some of her
> behavior could be likened to dropping a bomb and
> walking away before it went off. There was constant
> two-facing and backstabbing.
>
> One day, the head of HR and I were making
> rounds on the nursing unit and Bertha started
> yelling at her—her face flaming red with anger. Her
> bold, inappropriate communication was shocking to
> everyone who witnessed it. But, I learned later, this
> was not unusual for her.
>
> We had a frank conversation about what
> appropriate communication looked like, which was,
> of course, documented in her HR file. She went into
> high gear with her negativity after that—co-opting the
> previous nurses she had "mentored" into feeling sorry
> for her, and feeding into the "Poor me, I'm being
> picked on" mentality.
>
> I had already needed to counsel this nurse for

working outside her scope of practice once before, and she was shocked when she was on a final warning because of it, thinking it was "no big deal." She must have really thought we weren't serious because, not six months later, she sent a patient home without having discharge orders from the physician (who came looking for the patient on the unit)— literally practicing medicine without a license.

This was the last straw, and we moved quickly to terminate her. She was on duty when I told her I needed to meet with her. She sensed that something was "up," and said she wouldn't meet with us unless her husband was there with her. She was told, 'No, your husband isn't an employee—but you can identify another peer or employee to be present if you want someone to be here.'

Bertha continued to try to manipulate the situation so she could act like she was the one in control. She finally did ask another staff person to be present, with the full knowledge that the person would be privy to our entire discussion. She came in and we went through the final occurrence that had led us to this place. Bertha was very defensive, and thought that it was ridiculous that we thought discharging a patient without a physician's order was inappropriate.

Because she was known to have demonstrated an explosive, physically intimidating demeanor in the past, I had prepared by notifying security, so they could be present in the background in case they were needed, and to escort her to her locker and from the premises once we were done.

You would hope that it would end there. But nope, Abby added that Bertha wouldn't let go. She went to the union that was trying to organize the hospital to enlist their help. Bertha offered to be their "poster child."

Abby also reported something that is not all that uncommon. Bertha would continue to call the staff on the unit after she was gone. Even though Bertha was as disruptive as she was and had created a huge array of problems for co-workers over the years, many defended her ... "Poor Bertha, poor Bertha..." But, in time, the majority of staff started recognizing that their environment was so much more positive, and a sense of teamwork started to return—with the absence of Bertha's toxicity that had insidiously poisoned them over so many years. It was distressing to Abby that other leaders had been intimidated by Bertha for so many years, and had not taken the steps to put an end to this.

One of the most difficult things any leader has to do is terminate an employee. It takes courage and conviction, something that has to be used in dealing with staboteurs in any midst. And, something that leadership must pass on to its managers so that bad and underperforming employees can be let go.

Identifying the Staboteur

What if you are unsure as to who is creating chaos for you, or for the team? How do you identify the nasty people who create havoc in your life? Start by asking a few questions:

- *Does anyone encourage gossip?* Saboteurs and staboteurs are superb messengers and can hardly wait to pass on discrediting information.
- *Does anyone keep a tally sheet?* Staboteurs will keep track of your mistakes and share them with everyone.

- *Does information pass you by? Are you out of the loop?* Staboteurs isolate their targets from regular communication links.
- *Is anyone's job in jeopardy?* The past two decades have been an incredible breeding ground for change. When change occurs, anxiety and fear are its companions. Either creates a breeding ground for bad behavior.
- *Have new coalitions formed within your team or department?* Saboteurs and staboteurs switch friends and allies continually ... this week an employee seems close to another, the next week, only dust is left in their trail of friendship.
- *Does anyone routinely take the credit of others or discount them (or you and yours)?* Cheering and leading bravoes for anyone else's contribution to a project or idea is next to impossible. The only thing that really counts is that they get credit; who cares if they did the work or not?
- *Does anyone encourage others to take on tasks that appear impossible or extremely difficult?* The only reason they do is that they want the other person to fail ... the more public, the better. And they look "smart" for avoiding the task.
- *Is anyone too, too helpful?* Saboteurs and staboteurs will actually help others to the extent that their own work is not completed, yet visually it appears that they have time to spare to help someone who can't complete their own.
- *Is there anyone who would "profit" from someone else making a mistake?* Who isn't mistake free? Certainly not me, and I bet not you. And, haven't some of your greatest learning curves happened when a

mistake occurred? Staboteurs relish letting others know of any mishaps that occur ... their objective is to look better because they didn't do it. They may end up with your promotion, bonus, even your job.

- *Does anyone routinely bypass your authority?* You may think that you have no authority, but look closer. How can that be true? Every employee at every level has some level of authority. Decisions are made on an ongoing basis around efficiencies, how much time is allocated or left to complete tasks, or which rooms to start in. Even the housekeeper controls in which room the mop starts during her regular routine. Does anyone attempt to circumvent your routines—do they go over, under or around you to get their way?

- *Is there anyone who denies direct involvement ... yet knows all the details of a situation?* They may claim they "heard" it from others, but the uncovered facts usually reveal that they were somehow involved in the rumor creation, the conflict or whatever has occurred. After all, there's nothing like being on the front line to start the spillage of whatever dirt is out there or seeding the information flow.

As you went through the list above, could you tie someone's name to at least three of the situations identified? If so, you've got major warning signals flashing. There's a staboteur or saboteur in your midst. Pay attention.

Your workplace is a breeding ground for both. Men and women at all levels must learn to recognize, confront and then move to distance themselves from the encroachment on their professional and personal lives.

Managers routinely ignore problems, more out of fear of charges of sexism than anything else. The question becomes, "Why?"

Women are more likely to primarily sabotage and stabotage other women as 26 percent of our survey respondents reported. Men show no preference; they'll target either gender. When women mostly target other women, it is a form of gender harassment. Both problems are significant factors to the bottom line and must be addressed. Identify bad behavior; create programs to correct it; and, if unsuccessful in correction, terminate.

Dealing with Pit Bulls and the other critters is an important management issue. Diann Uustal, the author of *Clinical Ethics & Values: Issues & Insights in a Changing Healthcare Environment,* says,

> Excellence in nursing practice, individualized plans of care, positive patient outcomes, and creating a nourishing practice environment are desirable and achievable goals, but they are tinkling cymbals in the winds of change without a firm commitment to core health care values and value-based leadership! Management must insist on integrity. It leaves no doubt where you stand.

The health care workplace loses billions of dollars each year in lost productivity because of its unwillingness to deal with this issue in this way. It is about integrity and leadership. Just factor in the replacement costs of losing good employees when they finally throw in the towel and say, "Enough." Can your department or facility afford it?

Verbal Abuse ... Alive, Well and Deadly

Several years ago, I received a letter from Luther Christman, PhD, RN regarding a reference I made in my first book on women in health care, about symbolic cannibalism among nurses. As dean emeritus of Rush University College of Nursing, he felt that there were several reasons for it. He wrote,

> Bickering and backbiting begin in the beginning— education and service. Both are strongly separated from each other. There's a lack of real career commitment—most nurses have a series of part-time jobs instead of a true career. More education is needed, the majority of practicing nurses don't have a BSN. With powerlessness, other bad behaviors are bred.
>
> Nurses display tribal-like behavior, which is evidenced in the almost 100 national nursing organizations that destroy loyalty to the profession and to each other. A lack of racial and gender diversification exists in the primary women's professions.

Luther Christman has seen it all. He was the first to be honored as a "History Maker in Nursing" by the Center for the Advancement of Nursing Practice in 1992. He feels that the remnants of the Nightingale model have been an impediment to progress for nurses in general and that there is a "glass ceiling" for men in professions that have a high incidence of female employment.

Do Nurses Still Eat Their Young? ...
What Others Say

In the eighties, S. B. Freidman did a study focusing on relationships between nurses and physicians. She concluded that nurses were subjected to condescension, temper tantrums, scapegoating and public humiliation at the rate of six occurrences per month per nurse.

Helen Cox, the associate dean of Continuing Nursing Education at Texas Tech University Health Science Center for the School of Nursing in Lubbock, Texas, released her findings on verbal abuse among nursing personnel in 1987.

Her study's objective was to identify the frequencies, sources, nature of impact and possible solutions for verbal abuse. Burning out and exiting nursing were the primary results when conflicts developed between nurses and their peers and between nurses and both top level administrators and nursing administrators. In descending order, the culprits were physicians, patients, families of patients, and immediate supervisors, with 82 percent of the nurses stating that they had experienced verbal abuse.

Kathryn Braun, Donna Crisde, Dwayne Walker and Gail Tiwa-nak of the Queens Medical Center in Honolulu, Hawaii followed up Cox's work and decided to survey all registered nurses employed by the hospital in mid-1989 using Cox's original survey questionnaire. Abusive behavior was alive and well.

Instead of the reported dominant abuser being a physician, this study revealed that 80 percent of the staff experienced abuse from patients, 78 percent from a physician, 60 percent from a patient's family, 52 percent from staff nurses, 24 percent from immediate supervisors, 21 percent from subordinates, and 6 percent from administration.

Another study, post Cox's, was that of Suzanne Zigrossi, director of the Women's and Children's Center at Baptist Hospital in Miami, Florida. She found the predominant abuser was the patient, followed by the patient's family, physicians, peers and then supervisors—a slight variation from what Cox found. Types of behaviors included anger, disapproval, belittling comments, obscene language (usually from patients), name calling, rudeness, unreasonable demands, physical threats, sarcasm, sexual suggestions, condescending behavior, and ridicule.

Present day studies are now reflecting this shift, as I've found in my latest study. No longer is the physican the blatant jerk and abuser ... other nurses, patients (and their families) have become quite vocal and visible. And abusive.

In May, 2005, the *Journal of Nursing Management* reported on the work of Michelle Rowe and Holly Sherlock with St. Joseph's University in Philadelphia, Pennsylvania. Their theory was that nurses who were burned out would be more likely to abuse other nurses verbally. Indeed, they found that a fellow nurse would be the most frequent abuser (27 percent), followed by patients' families (25 percent), doctors (22 percent), patients (17 percent), residents (4 percent), other (3 percent) and interns (2 percent). When a nurse had been identified as the abuser, staff nurses were reported to be the most frequent target (80 percent) followed by nurse managers (20 percent).

In *Ending Nurse-to-Nurse Hostility*, author Kathleen Bartholomew wrote in 2006 that 60 percent of new RNs would exit their first positions within six months. Yikes! The cause: hostility in their workplace. It came from withholding information, verbal affronts, undermining and a variety of nonverbal innuendos.

New nurses were hung out there, game for the "nurses eat their young" syndrome. They have to be taught confrontation skills and managers must be savvy enough to recognize what's going on and deal with it. It's their responsibility to not allow bullying and hostility to breed.

Across the Pond, researchers with London University reported at the Royal College of Nursing's 2007 International Research Conference that almost half of student nurses on their work experience placements have been verbally abused.

In the London University study, Terry Ferns and Liz Meerabeau surveyed 114 student nurses in 2007. They found that 46 percent had reported they had been verbally abused by patients, relatives or staff. More than a third (39 percent) had seen other students being verbally abused and 61 percent said they were aware of other students experiencing verbal abuse. And, get this, 8 percent reported they had received death threats! Yikes!

JB's Keeper—

Verbal abuse, whatever the cause, has a negative effect on everyone. It's been linked to feelings of powerlessness, incompetence, low self-esteem and self-worth.

The Players ...

All of the following players take starring roles as being a staboteur in your midst.

Pit Bulls The key difference between the Pit Bull and the other players is her visibility and attitude. Pit Bulls will openly take credit for another's work and dare you to speak up; they will push and intimidate others into sticking their necks out in areas they have no business being in; and they think nothing of either stomping on or bypassing you to get their way. If a co-worker or manager walks like a Pit Bull, acts like a Pit Bull and barks/bites like a Pit Bull, no one needs an advanced degree in knowing what they are dealing with.

Skunks appear very visible and quite harmless. It's not uncommon to view them as sweet, almost syrupy in their mannerisms. You can't imagine them doing mean things ... yet they do. Given that Skunks prefer a covert operation to an overt, they work on keeping you disconnected and out of the information loop. They love gossip ... the odor of it spreading into every crevice of an organization.

Snakes strike when they feel their position or integrity is at risk. With the rampant change within health care, both clinical and behavioral skills are under the microscope. Lacking either, a Snake can evolve to distinction quickly. They do it by passing along rumors, discounting the work contribution of others, and enthusiastically encouraging a co-worker to take on something that no one in their right mind would.

Scorpions' overall attitude is to just make it through the day ... and for everyone to stay out of their way while they are doing it. They and the Slugs are the least aggressive when it comes to being overt. But, if something/someone irritates a Scorpion, that something/someone will pay for it. Gossip isn't their thing. They would more likely put a stinger in an accolade that has come your way, discount any authority you express, or act helpful until it no longer serves their purpose.

Slugs are the least aggressive of all the critters in the work-place. Their form of stabotage surfaces in appearing to help others, yet not doing their own work; participating in the gossip mill; and constantly shifting their workplace friendships. You may think you have an ally ... but that was last week.

Summing Up

Organizations continue to spend hundreds of thousands of dollars on marketing, sign-on bonuses and recruiting costs. How many of them truly do a realistic, probing exit interview to determine "why" someone quits? Is it because there is a better deal across town, another location? Is it because they feel that the new workplace they are going to is better? Are they being offered the opportunity for more training? Mentoring? Is the current workplace the pits? Why?

It would make far more sense to create a statistical model of why employees *really* quit so that problems, issues and bad behaviors can be dealt with instead of falling back on the usual excuse, "I'm leaving for more money" (rarely the case), and "I've got a job closer to home" (yes, at the hospital down the street). Too often, employees feel it's useless to tell the truth; that management doesn't really care nor will it do anything about it/her/him. Leaving and surviving become the chosen route.

For years, I've said that I wish I had $10 for every nurse and health care provider who had left their respective profession saying that they had had it—no longer would they be subject to the rotten and toxic behavior of their co-workers and of their management. I would be living on my own tropical island.

> ## JB's Keeper—
>
> *Better and wiser to keep the excellent employee*
> *than to lose her or him to a competitor or*
> *another industry because management failed*
> *to deal with the real cause of departure.*
> *The new workplace motto should be:*
>
> **Hire Slowly ... Fire Quickly**

Deteriorating situations exude negativity—contagious, insidious negativity. Once negativity has infected a deteriorating situation and become the "norm," its creates a domino factor. Every corner of the workplace is open to toxicity.

The Pit Bulls, Skunks, Snakes, Scorpions, and Slugs know the best breeding grounds. No organization is immune from conflict, even sabotage and stabotage. Because it does exist, there should not be a license or assumption that it be allowed (sometimes even encouraged by management's ignorance or benign neglect) to fester, to grow, to eventually take over an entire organization. If it does, forget about workplace shortages; extinction is on the way. The animals are in control.

4

Why Do These Critters Breed in Your Workplace? Because They Can....

There is a special place in hell
for women who don't help other women.
Madeline Albright on a Starbucks cup

W hy do workplaces, the female dominated ones, continue to report significant levels of women undermining other women—be it a co-worker or manager? Is there more conflict since the first study I did in 1987 or do people just grumble more about it than they did in the past?

Health care means caring. Rotten people and the behaviors they champion should be out of place and not welcome in the workplace. They aren't. The answer to the question, "Why do Pit Bulls, Skunks, Snakes, Scorpions and Slugs breed in your workplace?" is simply this: *because they are allowed to and can.*

The Problem

The increased reporting of undermining activity and conflict has multiple facets:

- The female dominated workplace
- A large percentage of women not wanting to work with other women
- An environment that now weighs behavioral and clinical skills as equal
- A rapidly changing work environment that continues to resist technology
- The increased necessity to understand and use technology
- Increasing resentment among older and/or senior employees when upfront moneys—bonuses—are paid to new hires
- Increased union organization activities, especially among nurses

The 2008 study indicated that over 26 percent of the women respondents did not want to work with or for another woman. Since 80 percent of overall health care employees are women, a potentially dangerous environment for both patients and working personnel is created.

Denial Is in Vogue ... Still

With the publication of *Woman to Woman* in 1987, many women's groups and associations were angry that I had pointed out the fact of these differences. It was said that women in the workplace should be viewed as equal with men, and that any discussion about differences or disparities would only hurt women in the end.

For some strange reason, that all changed in 2002. Publications such as *Woman's Inhumanity to Woman* by Phyllis

Chesler, *In the Company of Women* by Pat Hein and Susan Murphy, *Queen Bees & Wannabes* by Rosalind Wiseman and *The Secret Lives of Girls* by Sharon Lamb became the "talk" of the media ... and were met by denial by many professional women and organizations.

There are differences. To deny so is absurd. There is no question that women should have equal opportunity, and that women have the ability to do virtually any job on the *same level* as their male counterparts. That is a separate issue, however. The issue that I'm addressing is the fact that women don't always support other women. It permeates female-dominated professions, including nursing, dentistry, social work, teaching, secretarial services, real estate, banking and cosmetology.

Social Trends

Women have moved in growing numbers into higher-level positions. They make a lot more money. It's not uncommon for a nurse with an associate degree to make $50,000 plus within the first year of full-time work. Their employment has been a key factor in the shift toward services and away from manufacturing and industry.

Parity in the general paycheck has not yet occurred. It will only change when women are in sufficient numbers and are in the "pay-assignment" driver's seat—it doesn't matter what the industry is.

Only a few occupations pay at the same level for the same grade type for men and women—nursing and hygienists! In the eighties, women's earnings ranged from 60 to 64 percent of men's; in 1990, it increased to 70 percent; and in the first decade of 2000, there was little change. Women are continually getting more education, experience and recognition, and are moving into higher-level jobs. As women perform well in their new jobs, doors will continue to open for both entry and advanced levels. Recent statistics support this.

The Crab Crawl

Years ago, I was visiting my daughter when she lived in Maryland. We spent a beautiful Saturday at the shore, devouring one of my favorites, crab. When we selected ours to cook in the pots, I noticed that the baskets on the docks had no lids. Our cooker told us that they were never needed. "When one crab starts to crawl up, the others reach up to pull it down." That applies to the workplace as well. It's not uncommon to see a colleague start the professional climb and others reach out and attempt to pull her back.

Many of the women I interviewed in 1994 and again for this book reported that when they received promotions involving title and responsibility, they often found themselves in an "out group" environment. Colleagues and friends pre-promotion were now suspicious and distant. Girlfriend chat was a thing of the past.

Women who had broken out were not to be trusted ... they were now considered to be "one of them," whoever "them" is.

The service types of businesses have more women working in them than men. Therefore, a woman's most likely competitor is going to be another woman, especially in the early stages of her career.

Do Women Eat Their Young?

Women are still burdened with expectations and stereotypes of what they should do and how they should behave. These stereotypes specify that women should do certain types of work.

Although not directly related to health care, no one has to look further than the amount of dialogue, and downright hate, directed toward Senator Hillary Clinton, who at the writing of this first edition, was a contender for president of the United States. Tied with the failure to deal with and implement any type of health care reform in the eighties (forget about the nineties!), plus issues connected with Bill Clinton's presidency and I guess, just being a Clinton, the level of negativity directed towards her was unbelievably disproportionate to that of any of the other candidates, in either party.

In a column in the *New York Times* on February 10, 2008, Stanley Fish wrote,

> The responses to my column on Hillary Clinton hating have been both voluminous (the largest number in the brief history of "Think Again") and fascinating. The majority of posters agreed with the characterization of the attacks on Senator Clinton as vicious and irrational ...

He then continued with the statement that many of the posts agreed with him and then went on to rip her apart further. With phrases from women readers like,

> There's nothing to like about her ..."

followed by a significant number of negative remarks about her clothes, laugh, arrogance, ambition, power loving needs, and of course, her husband.

"It's obvious that she's had countless plastic surgeries ... after all, she's 60 and no one can look that good at 60," was a remark I overheard while seated at a table of 10 women at a conference in the Midwest.

Yikes! What's going on here? Who talks about men this way? And do men talk about women, and other men, the way Hillary's being blasted? Were the other candidates of all the parties being shredded the way she was? I don't think so.

As young girls, women are brought up to believe that they should be friends with everybody, and that friends don't usually compete with other friends. The premise is one of, "Be patient, your turn will come ..." Phooey, it's naïve to assume your turn will come; the fact is that more times than not, you've got to jump in and grab it. Otherwise, someone else will.

When it comes to friendships, they usually evolve over time. The reality is that not everyone is friend material.

The Bullier and the Bullette

Jane Stuart is director of OB and Women's Services at Catskill Regional Medical Center in Harris, New York. Originally a staff nurse, she's worn the management hat in a variety of areas for many years. Stuart has identified and defined what she calls the *Bullier* and the *Bullette* of the workplace.

Bulliers are experienced and basically tenured. They've seen it all and can tell you stories that go back to dinosaurian times. Stuart reported that one said to her,

> I have seen four VPs of Nursing come and go and I will still be here when this one goes. She's just the flavor of the month.

Stuart continues that the Bullier views the workplace as her turf and she's entitled to whip others into shape. She can browbeat, belittle and unmercifully find fault with anyone on the unit.

The Bullette is the nurse who has survived the Bullier's craft. She's developed an enabling relationship with the Bullier, and actually wishes she were her. It's her new role model. As Stuart says,

She's become a Bullier in training.

And, finally, Jane Stuart has come up with the Bullier-Bullette's Golden Rule:

It was done unto me and I shall do it unto you.

The above is a perfect illustration of a dysfunctional workplace—a too common health care workplace and the type of workplace where the Pit Bulls, Skunks, Snakes, Scorpions and Slugs flourish. Bulliers and Bullettes share a commonality with what has been observed by behaviorists: those who are abused (the Bullettes) turn into the abusers (the Bulliers).

Gender Stereotypes Have Challenges

Women managers and executives face a variety of tests. A laundry list of stereotypical perceptions and expectations of how they should behave is presented to them on a daily basis. It isn't unusual to find that the members of a work group will judge women more harshly when the women act in a more instrumental and analytical way, a style that is more characteristic of men. The same work group will be more positive when women act in a more expressive way, the expected female style.

My continuing research shows that many women feel compelled to downplay their strengths but must continue to display a tough shell in order to shake off the stereotypical view that they are too soft. Too female. Instead, they actually support the traditional male business method view that a rational, analytical style of management is always best—a style that, over time, unfortunately, will most likely be out of style.

Most women say they tend to do best with some form of the participative style of management, and current research continues to support that premise. Yet women who adopt it, and do what appears to work best, risk being stereotyped, since this is identified as the primary style of feminine leadership. Other observers believe that women do know how to work with people but lack important leadership skills: emotional stability, aggressiveness, self-reliance, analytical ability and objectivity—all qualities traditionally associated with men. It's no wonder that women managers feel great pressure to perform. It's a Catch-22 for them.

For 20 plus years, over a third of the women in my multiple studies have responded that, given their druthers, they would prefer to not work with other women. For the service industries, this is pretty devastating; most employees are female. As mentioned, this is certainly the case for health care.

Whether you have a dental practice with seven employees or a department in a large hospital with 300 employees, can you imagine one-third of them saying, "Nope, I'm not going to cooperate or work with you today...." The good news is that for the first time, seen with the most recent survey, the percentage has dropped to 26 percent—still a significant number, but a decrease finally after two decades of writing and speaking on this topic.

This is not a major issue for men; they've reported a much higher tolerance for working with women and being managed by women than women have. In some workplaces, there are still situations of adversarial relationships between women superiors and their female subordinates. These could be caused by the following:

- Women bosses may be demanding more of female subordinates, in order to mold them into competent managerial women.
- If a woman was in a staff position prior to moving into management, she may have higher expectations for staff she manages; after all, she knows where sloughing occurs.
- Staff could resent the additional demands and they may be disappointed that they aren't getting the warmth, support and encouragement commonly associated with their idea of a female boss.
- Women may suspect that there are a limited number of slots open to women, and so they feel competitive with their female bosses.

In some cases, conflicts occur when a younger woman supervises another who is senior in age.

Power Is Complex

Most large corporations and health care systems are highly complex, with many levels of power. Coalitions and factions in organizations are the norm. These groups serve two purposes: they provide a source of strength and nurturing, and they offer a power base for people working their way to the top. As individuals move from one group to another, they can easily step on others. If anyone is stepped on in the process, hostility and resentment can be a result.

All groups create their own cultural environments and worldviews. Anyone with low power in a group feels disappointed when her own values and opinions are not recognized. She in turn penalizes those who have even less power, and the pecking order goes into effect.

In one organization I consulted with, it was clear early on that status had a great deal to do with conflict and undermining in the all-female administrative assistant work area. If one woman worked for a senior executive Vice President and another, who worked for just a vice president, needed a file, the higher status administrative assistant would drag her feet in getting the info to her.

Another problem surfaces: since there are fewer women running hospitals or at senior corporate levels, women in these positions are more visible. Think of the women in the Senate of the United States—they only represent 15 percent of all the senatorial seats. When the senators Clinton, Snowe or Feinstein take a position, all eyes turn toward them, where if it was a male (assuming he isn't running for president), it would be more ho-hum.

Power Squeezes

The women in leadership and management are in a unique situation. Their power links are stretched. Demands of senior administration have to be met; and at the same time, they have to contend with the resistance of employees who may resent being stuck in their lower-opportunity positions. There could be resentment that they've moved up and gotten ahead.

Stabotage and sabotage kick in. Passive-aggressive actions surface, such as slacking off, not being available or ignoring routine requests. When the manager responds to these actions, she's deemed demanding, critical and pushy. The cycle is set in motion ... the more the manager puts pressure on the employee, the more she's viewed as a shrew.

In health care, if there is sabotage and stabotage in play, the odds are that women will more likely target their own gender. Since there are a disproportionate number of women to men, there are more females to target. Everything is more exaggerated than in a more balance- and gender-integrated workplace.

Patient Misuse of Power

When *Zapping Conflict in the Health Care Workplace* was initially published, it revealed that patients, and sometimes their families were abusive ... way ahead of any negativity reported elsewhere about physician-related abuse.

This is a challenge that health care professionals face almost on a daily basis, and it's global. In 2008, the Health Ministry of China stepped up to the plate and published rules that guarded the rights of nurses that would give them "protection" against any violent attacks by patients and/or their families.

In 2006 alone, over 10,000 attacks on hospital staff had been reported there. The new order from the State Cabinet in Beijing states that, "Anyone who impedes nurses from performing their duties or who insults, threatens or assaults them, must be punished according to the law."

Summing Up

In today's workplace, management leans toward a more personal and participative style, creating a more humanistic and supportive environment for workers. This is a good thing. One benefit is increased productivity and increased loyalty, but this environment can also be a breeding ground for sabotage and stabotage.

There isn't a workplace that doesn't have difficult people who vent their feelings and hostilities toward one another. Pit Bulls, Skunks, Snakes, Scorpions and Slugs are more likely to reinvent the rules of the workplace, forming them into whatever seems to be expedient and effective at any given time.

When patients and their families are abusive, even acting as bullies, to nurses and other health care professionals, management can't bury its head. When health care professionals are abusive, even acting as bullies, to co-workers, management, patients and families, management can't bury its head.

When abusive behavior is ignored and over-looked, the clear statement that is delivered is that it's OK to continue with it. A "no-tolerance" position has to become the operative motto.

5

Gossip, Backstabbing & Friendship ... Oh My!

> Whoever shares gossip with
> you will gossip about you.
> *Dr. Judith Briles*

Women like to talk. They talk about a huge variety of things, including very personal stuff. Stuff which, in many cases, certainly should be left out of any discussion with someone who would be considered just a casual acquaintance.

With more than one-quarter of our survey respondents stating a preference not to work with other women, there are going to be problems. In some workplaces, that preference can be life threatening. In the case of nursing, if one nurse doesn't like another nurse or puts her in a category of "lesser importance," a call out for assistance for a patient can be ignored resulting in harm.

In others, it can be more of a nuisance. It may take longer to get something out of a clerk to complete your project if she doesn't cater to (or respect) you. Or, it could fall in-between—you may end up looking incompetent to others because you either don't have full cooperation of your team or you are unable to gather critical information because it's been road blocked by a co-worker who refuses to supply necessary information.

When women work with other women, confusing friendship with friendliness can and does create mayhem. Women too easily cross the line. Most work friendships should remain within the work-related environment. Going out with other women for a drink or playing in the summer softball or volleyball league continues the "work" flavoring. The crossover to family and more personal activities can complicate the picture.

This doesn't mean that all female relationships should be stopped and not extended to your personal "other" life. It does mean that you need to be careful that friendships are privileged and are built and earned over time. Imagine a workplace romance. Few people meet and instantly fall in love; most relationships develop over time. The great majority of positive, caring and growing relationships have substantial investments of time in them.

Loose Tongues Sink Jobs

Who would have thought that a small town known for its presidential campaigns and retail shops would make national headlines on the topic of gossip?

In 2007, the Town Council of Hooksett, New Hampshire fired four women from their jobs for starting a rumor about their boss, David Jodoin, and another co-worker. They spread rumors, and lies, that he was catting around and having an affair. As rumors do, this one grew and multiplied. The Mrs. wasn't too pleased when she heard them, nor were her friends—and certainly their boss was upset.

When the rumors landed at the Town Council, action happened. The four women were fired for gossiping. Hooksett, NH was now noted for another form of politics: office politics.

The women's response was basically what's the big deal? The local paper took a survey on readers' attitudes about gossip. Only nine percent thought they should be sacked. The rest were more tolerant ... after all, most people do gossip in some form so it must be OK.

The rumor was untrue, and the four women admitted that they made it up. They sued the Council to get their jobs back and saw no harm in what they had done.

Gossiping Can Be Brutal

On the low end of the spectrum, gossiping can be embarrassing for the victim. Escalating, it can easily lead to bullying, defamation of character, loss of reputation and job.

When it comes to gossiping, rarely is the gossip positive and done to shed a positive light on someone. In its casual form, it's usually based on unsubstantiated reports and negative remarks about the target.

When it comes to work-related gossip with outsiders, it can be viewed as a breach of confidentiality, which workers owe to their employer. Work gossip can affect customers and sales.

Dr. Scott LeBuke's dental practice is in British Columbia, Canada. He takes gossip, and office gossip, very seriously. He views gossip as destructive to his practice and his patients, even going so far as not carrying any of the celebrity-type "gossip" magazines like People, InTouch, or Entertainment. His attitude is,

Why have anything around that will only seed it?

You may not think that gossip is drastic or violent. But, think of it this way. It can destroy lives. It is a birthing ground for contempt and distrust among co-workers. When distrust is rampant, productivity and employee morale nosedive.

A caution for women surfaces. It's very common for women to share personal information. Sometimes, they literally reveal information about themselves that can become self-generated gossip or seed someone else's fertile imagination. Men gossip as well. But their form is less likely to carry the more intimate details that women offer.

Chitchat or Defamation?

So, what's the difference between "harmless" chitchat and "harmful" chitchat? When does it cross the line to blatant destructiveness?

Bad gossip leads to defamation of character—when creating false rumors and spreading them, the creator knows that they are untrue or thinks they may be untrue, but what the heck, passes them on anyway. People can and do sue for defamation of character ... is doing it worth it?

Stepping Aside ...

Just before my first book was published in 1981, Carole Hyatt, author of *Shifting Gears* and *When Smart People Fail,* and I were the speakers on a cruise in the Caribbean. I was excited with the pending debut and Carole was sharing some of her "author" wisdom with me.

Within our group of approximately 75 women, one woman stood out and quickly became the topic of "discussion" when we recessed at the end of the day.

As the chatter accelerated, drowning out our conversation, Carole finally said, "I'm uncomfortable with what is being said here. I would love to stay and be with you all, but I don't want to talk like this about her. If you would like me to stay, we need to change the discussion."

Long pause ... then the conversation shifted. I never forgot the looks on the many faces. And to this day, I keep Carole's words in my mind, "I would love to stay and talk ... but not like this..."

It takes someone to speak up or out and say, "not this, not now." Yes, I know that idle gossip can sometimes be fun and entertaining. But it can be so hurtful.

So, what do you do? The smartest thing is just to steer clear of gossip. Dump the media pieces about what Brad and Angelina or Britney are up to. I suspect you are entertained by some of the nonsense that is reported, but truth be told, is this essential to your work, your life, your family?

Gossiping as Sport

Gossip is the number one way to undermine another. It's insidious in the workplace. Contrary to popular belief, it's not an exclusive with women; men do it as well. There is a difference though. Women tend to be more probing and to obtain more personal information that can be spread about.

June is the director of a women's health floor in a hospital with 400 plus beds. When she was clinical nurse specialist in Obstetrics, gossip was like the numbing background of Muzak in the unit. She feels that there is no worse gossip than what is heard on an OB floor. Her take ...

A lot of gossip was around sexuality and sex. Some of the jokes were funny. I wasn't married, nor was I dating at the time. I'm straight and had never done anything to indicate otherwise, but I was the butt of jokes on my floor. I remember one time a nurse came up to me and said, 'June, you're just like the slogan for 7-Up: you never had it, and you never will.' And then she started laughing out loud in front of all the other women in our department. I was so angry and stunned, all I could do was cry.

When gossip is circulating, rarely is the benefit of doubt given—people love to think the worst, not the best— which is usually the mission of gossip ... and the gossiper. Gossip is usually counterproductive and can be extremely negative.

What is gossip? Simply this ...
Any negative conversation of fact or rumor, that is of an intimate or personal nature when the targeted person who it is about is not present.

Years ago, *Self* magazine surveyed its readership, asking if they gossiped. A significant percentage responded that they did. The follow-up question asked who the subject was, giving a checklist to select from—celebrities, family, and friends were all on the list. When the responses were tallied, friends led the list. "Why?" was the final question. Because it was "fun" was the number one response.

What woman hasn't visited a salon for a hair styling? While waiting for the appointment or during a treatment, what is she reading there? Most likely, it won't be self-improvement or business magazines. It will be the gossip rags—*Us, People, InStyle,* anything celebrity driven. You may think, "Well, what's the harm...?" Merely this ... once you start on the path of reading about other people's flaws, screw-ups, divorces, etc., it sets up a negative spiral. Something that is casual can easily become a full-grown habit. Not a good thing.

Gossip is bad news indeed. When you are doing the gossip, it implies ...

- You make judgments, usually without facts behind them.
- You don't respect others.
- You don't want others to respect you.

Not respect you? If you blab and talk about anyone to others, rest assured, you will go down a notch or two in their eyes. If you betray a confidence that has been told to you directly or you pass on information that is half-baked or downright untrue, you become someone to stay away from. Any creates steps to disrespect for self.

Savvy and non-toxic workplaces (and relationships) strive to create a no-tolerance zone. Be gossip free. Yes, I know that gossiping can be "fun" just as the Self survey implied, but it can also be incredibly harmful. You can start by removing items from offices and waiting areas that are conducive to gossip—the magazines and papers that increase their circulations by blabbing about anything and anyone. Choose to be gossip free.

JB's Keeper—

The tongue only weighs a few ounces ... yet so few can hold theirs. Don't get caught up in the rumor mill. Delete rumor creators, rumor carriers and gossip from your circle of "friends." They aren't.

"Inside" the Staboteur

Staboteurs aren't confident women. They can be viewed as bullies and betrayers. They build their "fake" confidence by putting others down, by passing malicious gossip, taking credit or discounting another's contributions. Sometimes they are downright mean.

They often get others to confide in them. As in fishing, once they "hook" another, the reeling begins. I've been in workplaces where the staboteur is finally terminated and co-workers end up wearing arm bands—a show of grief for the "dearly departed."

What gives? Most likely, seduction. It's not uncommon for staboteurs to seduce colleagues into joining up ... bad-mouthing, discounting work, gossiping, and generally disruptive workplace harmony. Think of a prison—gangs are common. Inmates join in, seeking protection from other gangs.

In the workplace, even though the other gang may be the "good guys," the staboteur preys on the less confident—no workplace has 100 percent highly confident and achieving employees. Staboteurs know this and seek out the others to bond with ... even control.

While I'm Away ...

Edward Smolak is the admitting manager for Sunnyside Community Hospital in Washington state. The staff is primarily women, as most are in the hospital environment. Several had approached him in his office with complaints about others. His awareness of the increased levels of gossip, bickering and complaining finally came to a head as he was planning his winter vacation. He noted that it was weaving into other areas of his organization. As he readied for his vacation, he sent a memo to everyone on the admitting team. His words ...

I am becoming increasingly concerned about the level of gossiping, bickering, and complaining going on amongst our Admitting Department Staff. There is no positive outcome whenever department staff gossip, complain or bicker about other department staff or about others within the hospital.

It only creates bad morale and only breeds resentment throughout the department as well as the entire organization. Your co-workers do not have a need to hear anyone bring down anyone. Moreover, our patients and customers do not need to hear any of this inappropriate behavior.

If anyone has an issue with another individual, he/she should confront that individual privately and respectfully in an attempt to resolve those issues. If anyone has any issues regarding me, they should only direct those issues directly to me and give me the courtesy of trying to address their issues. Your co-workers do NOT need to be the recipients of your issues and concerns regarding me or others whom you are dissatisfied with.

If, after confronting the party you have an issue with, you are not satisfied with their response, then come to me and I assure you we will meet to address your issue or concern and come up with a resolution. Unresolved issues and concerns only fester over time and only lead to resentment and breakdown of team morale.

Whew ... how would you like to get a memo like that? It takes courage for a manager to lay things out and confront them head-on. Smolak shares that he's been back several months now, and he can note a significant change within the department. People are more pleasant to each other and the level of complaining and bickering has dramatically been reduced.

The outcome for the organization can be measured as well. Patients and customers have ears. They know when there's grumbling and complaining going on. No one should be subjected to it ... ever.

If he hadn't addressed the issue prior to his leaving, guaranteed, the brewing would have notched up to a level that would have most likely resulted in a few people saying, "Enough, I'm out of here."

Don't Get Sucked In ...

Gossip isn't just about others; it could be about you. That hurts. You could be the intended subject of gossip. You could also be so caught up in it that you become the carrier. Computers are as commonplace as a toilet. The speed, and damage, done through an e-mail is far-reaching. Plus, it's not by mouth, there's a written record to show that you might be behind it. With the Internet, your rule should be that nothing is private ... nothing.

Be cautious with what you openly tell others about yourself. In minutes, those words could be everywhere. Is that what you would want? Your personal and professional persona is at risk. Be mum about the hot date you had, how screwed up your kids or spouse are; your unhappiness with your present job, mistakes and screw-ups that have caused you grief in the past, and especially how rotten you think some of your co-workers or boss are.

When it comes to gossip, think about politics and corporate PR clean-up campaigns. The spin factor comes into play ... people tweak and alter what they hear, either from non-clarity or to juice it up a bit. What you hear from another may have no relation to the truth.

> ## JB's Keeper—
>
> *As girls, many of us grew up with the advice from Mom to be friends with everyone. Mom was and is wrong. What Mom should say is, "Not everyone is friend material— there are plenty of jerks and jerkettes out there. Be cautious when sharing any information."*

Building Positive Relationships

In a collaborative workplace where women are working together, good things happen. Team members speak up, compete, confront and work in partnership—all actions that are the building blocks of healthy relationships.

As an office manager in a dental practice with six dentists, Susan noticed significant changes as soon as women dentists began to join the practice. Prior to that, she didn't see a lot of doctor-patient interaction. For her, women dentists have made a difference ...

The female dentists tend to refer their patients for additional information, have more follow-ups, and tend to be more open about the whole concept of providing dental care information to their patients. Women dentists champion education. They want to teach their patients to be more aware and to be a part of making decisions about their own care. In the past, the male doctors didn't focus on that.

In the NCIU, Martha has seen impressive changes in doctor and nurse dynamics. She echoes Susan's experience in the dental office ...

Women doctors have improved our workplace. They are more down to earth, less godlike, and have an incredible work ethic. They actually honor and respect the nursing staff. In our unit, they strive for collaboration on the different issues involving our tiny patients. The male doctors are still handing down edicts and telling us what to do. The women doctors seek our input.

I'm sick of the temper tantrums that are routine with the male docs; they blame nurses for their own screw-ups, write derogatory comments to them on order sheets and think nothing of berating a nurse in front of anyone. One complained to the director of nursing about a nurse who called him about a patient and then recorded key points of their conversation on the progress notes on the patient's chart. The doctor was incensed that she had done so without his permission.

Annabelle is fairly new to nursing. On the floor for three years, her reaction to women doctors: it's just easier. She shares,

There is a much more relaxed relationship—more of a camaraderie with the women, versus working with the male doctors. With a man, you have to approach him correctly and make it look like *it's* his idea, whatever it is, even though you planted it in the first place. With the women doctors, it's totally different.

You just state the way you think it ought to be, and
they just say yes or no. We don't have the
confrontations and conflicts that we routinely have
with the male doctors. Egos are put aside.

All this sounds good, but it's not always so wonderful.
Some of the women doctors indicated that not everything
was perfect in their working relationships with nurses.
Naomi is now an MD; prior to that she was a surgical
nurse. Her observation is that there is more friction ...

I've seen envy from some of the nurses toward other
female health care workers. I believe it comes from
their non-understanding of why another female in the
hospital has more power than they do.
    The public also makes wrong assumptions. They
expect to see women as nurses or lab technicians, but
not doctors. It's not that they dislike it. Rather, they
just don't recognize that we are there.

Does geography play a role in gender attitudes? In the
South, many of the survey respondents reported that the
expectations around the women (doctors and staff) were a
gender issue. It's not uncommon for patients to expect a
woman doctor to act like a nurse, and for that matter, to
be the nurse—to be softer and caring, not to give orders or
tell them what they have to do.
    One of the women doctors I spoke with practices in
Georgia. Her take on male and female differences ...

I don't see a lot of the support for the female
doctors that the nurses give to the men. It may
be a competitive thing. I think a lot of the nurses

view themselves as rivals with the women doctors, not as their support team. They are far more inclined to help the men.

As the secretary to the director of nursing for 15 years, Anne hears a lot of the hospital scuttlebutt. She is interested in the changes that the female physicians have brought to her workplace. Anne says that there is a difference in the newer physicians and how they interact with the staff. Her experience ...

> The first round of physicians had to really fight their way through school. Their attitude with the staff is more likely to be 'I'm the doctor, and you're the nurse.' The newer generation of women has a different take. They work with the nursing staff using a more team-oriented approach. I feel the younger generation of doctors will change our workplace for the better.

Medical and dental schools are close to 50/50 with male and female candidates—some even have a higher female percentage. Many of the top-rated nurses who've been in nursing for decades would most likely have chosen the physician or dentist path if it had been open to them. Today it is. And, some of those nurses and hygienists actually went back to school and became physicians and dentists.

MaryAnn, a nursing supervisor, talked about one of her hospital's physicians, who used to be an RN ...

> Many grumbled that she was more demanding of the nurses. They even called her a bitch. She probably is more demanding. She knows what the work expectations are and she knows what goofing off and dragging feet look like. After all, she has been in

their shoes. Since she's only been out of medical school for a few years, she watches herself, because she doesn't want to screw up. If she does, it reflects on all of them.

MaryAnn added that the other women are more likely to speak up about and against the women doctors than they are the men. She also noted that it was the women physicians who were more likely to be called for emergencies than their male counterparts. She continued,

It's more common for the male doctors to not work off-hours or overtime. Sports and other activities are their preferences. The nurses didn't bother to call them; they would just call the women doctors.

I've also noted that the women doctors are not as quick to jump on the nurses or reprimand them for not coming to their rescue and helping them out as would the male doctors. The women patients love the female physicians. They feel that they understand what they need.

MaryAnn also is a believer that women doctors listen more effectively than their male counterparts ...

I find it very refreshing to have female physicians. They bring a whole different twist to how we interact with our patients. These ladies don't make any bones about a situation. If they think something isn't right, they are more inclined to say, 'Cut the bull crap.' They talk to the nurses as human beings, and they understand some of the frustrations we experience with patients as people, not just as bodies with an illness. When they call someone a jerk, the label fits.

Sharon has worked in general dentistry practice for many years. Besides the regular patients, her office also cares for hygienists and dental assistants. Her take on male-female differences includes ...

I believe a lot of older women still prefer working for a man. Part of it is age. I know for me it's much easier to work with people my age or younger than to work with people who are older.

When I worked for a male dentist as an employee dentist, the dental assistant and staff, all women, would work for him but not for me. I remember asking one of the assistants to do something for me. She just left the room. I believe it's a generational thing. Older women prefer working for a man, and his age doesn't matter. They feel much more comfortable.

They used to get really ticked off when my patients called me by my first name. It's never been a big deal to me to be called Doctor, but to them it was very important. The woman who is now my partner is nine years older than I am. She believes that patients should call her Doctor. Mine call me Sharon.

Creating and Building Respect

Today's generation of female doctors is far more positive and intuitive about their support staff than the women physicians and dentists who completed their training more than 15 years ago.

Martha is representative of many of the women doctors we interviewed. She recalls being a resident and doing a surgical rotation with another woman in a large university-affiliated hospital. Most nights were tough, but at times she was actually able to get five to six straight hours of sleep. Angela, her fellow resident, wasn't so successful. Martha revealed ...

> Angela is a wonderful person. But she could push the button of any nurse. Her surgical rotation started a few weeks after mine. Within days, she complained she was getting dumb phone calls all through the day and night and that the nursing staff was a royal pain in the ass. Truth be told, they were getting back at her for pissing them off. The first rule I learned is keep the nurses on your side. They are the ones who really have the power around here. Once you piss them off, you're dead.

Health care professionals must understand that everyone on the team—nurses, assistants, other support staff and the doctors themselves each are an intricate part of the team. The best way to work with others is to respect them as individuals and for the talent they bring. Through the years, Martha has observed male interns, residents and specialists handing down orders. Their style is more dictatorial. Unfortunately, she says, some of the women doctors behave the same way the men do. She continues,

> I have a great deal of respect for nurses. We couldn't do what we do without them. At times, though, I believe the women doctors and nurses get into a type of competition. I've also been on the receiving end, when nurses sometimes had a problem accepting orders from me. It's only from the female nurses that I have had problems, when I've given orders

and they haven't wanted to take them. When I observed their interactions with the male interns and residents, I didn't see the problems that I had over the same issue.

There are times when there will be competition between women in the workplace. Martha feels that when the competitive spirit surfaces, the best way to resolve the problem is to acknowledge it, then defuse it. Her way is to actively work with the nurses and reinforce the fact that they are on her team. Her solution ...

When I did my first internship, it was in a neonatal nursery. I'd never even been in a neonatal nursery before, much less worked in one. There were nurses who had worked there for over 15 years. The reality was they could run that nursery just fine without me—they knew more than I did. I would have been an idiot to think that I always knew what was best. Anytime that orders needed to be written, I got into the habit of sitting down with whoever the nurse was and saying, "What do you think?"

Doctors who don't think they can learn from nurses will only sabotage themselves and their patients. I think most nurses are dynamite. I can't tell how many times I've had my tail saved by good nurses over the years.

Building a workplace that is woven with respect and collaboration is not something that is done overnight. It takes time, even years. When individuals are treated with respect—be they co-worker, manager or patient—their diversity is honored and their lives and work fill with integrity. It becomes a workplace of choice.

The Players ...

Pit Bulls are aggressive in their attempts to create friendships and maintain them. They don't have many and the ones that are in their select circle are kept on a short lease. Friends of Pit Bulls are expected to be followers, not the initiator of ideas—be they within the workplace or outside of it.

In many workplaces when the Pit Bull resigns or is terminated, it's common to experience a "mourning" among the few friends left behind. Friends might wear black bands on their arms. After all, she (or he) acted as a buffer, and in some cases, as the blocker in protecting them from others.

When Pit Bulls work in a pack, a non-Pit Bull who gets sucked into a quasi-friendship will eventually get bitten herself. Pit Bulls flex their imaginary muscles with workplace friendships. It's a "do as I do/say/am."

Skunks are shy, look harmless and are sometimes downright cute. Caution should be in order. Skunks react from fear of the unknown. With friendships, sometimes uncertainty surfaces. Communication snafus and misunderstandings can cause anxiety, not a good thing to do with a Skunk. Their defensive reaction is quick, almost uncontrollable. The odor left behind permeates every nook and cranny.

Snakes and their friends have challenges. When a friendship with a Snake is engaged, the Snake has the capability of coiling around and strangling the life out of the relationship. You may know who the Snakes are, yet feel (and have experienced) overall positive interaction with them. But, and it's a big but, if you speak out against them or question their motives, expect a strike from them in some form.

You may not initially see an attack coming, but you will definitely feel their fangs ... be it questioning your credibility and professional skills or poisoning your relationships with others in the workplace.

Scorpions create interesting friendships. On the surface, everything may appear copasetic. But, if something raises the tail of a Scorpion, anyone who gets in their way will feel the sting. Friendships with Scorpions are not long term. At some point, the stinger comes out; it's the nature of the beast.

Slugs are safe. They have minimal expectations of their friends, making few, if any demands in the relationship. Slugs are the safest friendship to have with the bad girls and boys of the workplace. Slugs don't like to make waves and would prefer to be left alone. One of the key drawbacks when aligning with a Slug is the ooze factor ... their low energy, low drive, low everything rubs off. Hanging with a Slug will most likely turn you into one.

Summing Up

Women can work productively and effectively with other women. At the same time, they can compete and be assertive without viewing all other women as rivals and enemies. They can be supportive, and friendships can evolve.

When women are confident about who they are and what they are, there's not a problem with other women stretching, reaching and growing. It will be women, not men, who redefine what it means for women to work with women.

It's not self-improvement ... it's self-awareness ... followed by self-commitment to change ... and finally implementing the desired change. It's the only way one can change.

6

Unwritten Rules ... the **Real** Culture of Today's Workplace

> Everything we do,
> every decision we make and
> course of action we take is based
> on our consciously and unconsciously
> chosen beliefs, attitudes and values.
> *Dr. Diann Uustal*
> *Caring for Yourself ~ Caring for Others*

Within a short distance inside the main door of any workplace will be a plaque or framed statement ... the *mission* of the organization. They are often created with the guidance of a professional facilitator. Groups and boards sometimes take months to find just the right words to use as their guiding light and principle on how the business/organization reaches out to the community and operates.

These mission statements and codes of ethics always sound fabulous. Definitely well meaning and, if practiced to a tee, every workplace would be the place to be.

With that said, if every workplace truly practiced its Code of Ethics and Mission statements, this chapter would end here. It obviousely doesn't.

JB's Keeper—

The way people treat other people, whether it is within the workplace, between co-workers and management and/or its customers, is really the practicing code of ethics and how the people interpret the workplace's mission statement.

Unwritten Rules Rule

Every workplace has them. Sometimes there are different rules for different status, length of employment, even who you are aligned with! Some are obvious, others incredibly subtle.

There are two identifiable rules in the workplace: go to work, and do the job. It's the 100 plus unwritten rules that can destroy your working relationships and your work environment.

Most rules are commonsensical, but when the unwritten rules are not followed, they seed discontent. A single incident may not seem *important*, but over a period of time, many small infractions can make life a monstrous hassle.

Examples of simple unwritten rules include in the coffee room: the first person in makes the first pot, and the person who takes the last cup of coffee makes a new pot. Another: in the copy room, if someone switches from regular to legal size paper, switch back to regular for the next person; or if someone uses fuchsia paper for a flyer, the unwritten rule is to switch back to white. You know, commonsense courtesies. Easy.

But now it gets dicey. In an ongoing exercise I do in all of my *Zapping Conflict* workshops, I break the group into clusters and have them brainstorm unwritten rules—the things that you wished you had known *before* working; the ones that you stumbled across by accident or mistake, the ones that you could have been chewed out for if violated, or ones that are even used as a "test" to see if you have the right stuff to be on the team.

Participants are told to think about areas of the workplace—housekeeping, co-workers who have kids, vacations and holidays, protocols, use of space, as well as dealing with different members of staff and departments, interpreting and understanding mannerisms of others, identifying territories, or even working with customers and patients. There is no area closed off from inclusion.

The assignment lasts 15 to 20 minutes. Some of the rules are outrageously funny, some outrageously ridiculous and some outrageously scary or downright mean. The examples are shared with the group and they are recorded on poster-sized paper and displayed for all to see. It's not uncommon to hear tons of laughter, even booing at some of them—it's also common to see heads nodding and hear words of agreement about how good or bad or mean they are.

Some workshop participants are stymied, not able to think of anything; others fill a page quickly. One way to start the ball rolling is simply to ask ... "Has there ever been a time when you thought, or even said outloud, I wish someone had told me that." What was the "that" ... it could be as simple as not using someone's mug.

Many of the responses I've received over the years can't be included because of space—there are thousands of them. And, sometimes they are so unique to the organization, that they must remain undisclosed to others.

Here's an interesting one: at my Zapping Conflict workship during an annual meeting of a state hospital organization a few years ago, we all roared when some said that Sister Mary hated the color red, so that if you had a meeting with her, you learned quickly not to wear the color. Now, if you were a staboteur, you could easily say to someone, "Oh, don't forget to wear your red power suit at your meeting with Sister Mary tomorrow."

Some unwritten rules are general, such as ...

Temps always get the heavy work or worst assignments
Don't take responsibility for peers; grumble instead
The previous shift doesn't have to complete its work
If there is a mistake, blame it on the student or new hire
New employees must pay their dues
Last person in gets the worst assignment
Don't expect to have the same patient everyday
Don't say "oops"
Support all decisions of the team, even if you disagree
Don't air the team's dirty laundry
If it's not documented, you didn't do it
Doing extra work is brownnosing
Don't be a whistleblower
Don't challenge authority
No handwritten signs
Put the seat down
Squeaky wheel gets her way

No one can drink coffee if the supervisor is present
Don't use someone else's coffee cup
Don't unplug equipment
Speak your native tongue in the lounge
Don't talk to patients in the hallway
First one in turns the lights on; last one out turns
    them off
Don't read newspapers or magazines at your desk
Don't touch someone's computer without permission
If you smoke outside, pick up your cigarette butts
Come to work even when sick—spread it around
Food left around is free game
If you didn't bring food, you don't share in the potluck
English should only be spoken at nurse's station
When there are certain re-admits—run
Don't leave things undone for the next shift
Smokers can take more breaks than nonsmokers and
    get away with it
Certain people get specific time slots for lunch and
    dinner
Listen when someone is talking
Don't argue in front of co-workers or patients
Too many bathroom breaks are frowned on
If you are sick, you get the silent treatment when
    you return
Parents can be on the phone more than nonparents
Parents get certain holidays off
Parents don't have to work overtime; can come in late;
    leave early
Parents can take more sick days off
It's OK to be late
No more than two Fridays off in a row
If you take a risk, you had better be right
You get feedback only when you grumble

Others, more colorful ...

Whoever is stuck with the narcotic keys has to do the
  report
Don't piss off a member of a clique
Don't sleep at work
Don't identify a problem because you will have to come
  up with the solution
If you understand the form, management will change it
Screen calls at home (they may want you to come in
  to work)
Don't wear thong underwear with white pants
Avoid "Bertha" at all costs
Rotate difficult patients with difficult RNs
Give laxatives at the end of your shift
Nurses with false fingernails don't have to do
  patient care
Flush the toilet all the way down
Don't sit in anyone's favorite chair
It's OK to eat patient's food
Always be nice to tech support
If you have to see Sister Mary, don't wear red
Don't walk behind Dr. Smith when rounding

Rules that have surfaced have numbered in the thousands. Some unique to a specific workplace/industry; others more universal. Many are profound, extreme or deeply
disturbing, and some downright silly.

Have you ever been in a situation and you wondered,
"Why do we do it this way?" The answer is usually, "Because,
we've always done it that way." Or maybe, "Well, since
Bertha worked here ... that's the way it's been done." You
may wonder who Bertha is ... who knows, she doesn't work
there anymore!

What Unwritten Rules Do You Work Under?

In the South, I did a program on-site for a facility that required all personnel within women's services to attend. Seems that the Pelvic Palace, the money-generator for the hospital, was at war between days and evenings, not to mention delivery and postpartum care. The new director was being dumped on by the old-timers.

When I introduced the identifying unwritten rule activity, all were enthusiastic. That was, until we really got into it. One of the unwritten rules that surfaced after a few minutes dealt with new people: It was OK to be rude ... to "test" them to see if the new hire had the "right stuff."

The staff had declared a silent war on the new director from the moment she arrived. When she toured the units in her capacity, staff literally turned their backs on her as she approached. Brats.

The unwritten rule was that rudeness was OK, that Southern hospitality was a myth, and it didn't matter that she was the "new" boss.

After two days on-site, staff agreed to try some new things. To open up communication channels at all levels. To stop playing the silly and mean games that had been the norm. And, they were told that if there wasn't a significant behavior and attitude adjustment, they would be given the door.

So many times, management and administration fails to measure what the cost of a disruptive employee is. Too many times, "stars" are not the stars that management perceives them to be. Their attitudes and work styles may actually lower productivity, morale and teamwork of others. Some good nurses will resign and go to work for competitors. Turnover increases. Management's unwritten rule to keep their "stars" at almost all costs often turns out to be a major financial and workforce loss.

Unrealistic Unwritten Rules

Jenny works in a large dental practice with eight dentists and another 40 staff to support the busy practice. She loves her work, but not what some of her colleagues do to others. At times, she feels she would be better off if she could work in a vacuum because she has seen so many awful things the old-timers do to new employees—the games they play.

Jenny feels strongly that established staff should open up during orientation so that anyone new will understand all the nuances of what is expected of them. If one of the unwritten rules is to blame "it," whatever it is, on the new hire, her workplace is a perfect example. Jenny adds,

> The older assistants expect a lot more of the newer ones. Everyone makes mistakes, especially when you are unfamiliar with the practice and certainly new within a dentistry practice. Why they expect them to know all the rules, all the requirements, and all the personalities of everyone is beyond me. There is a lot of bitching going on, and there are times I do not know why I do what I do. I love what I do; I just wish the atmosphere was better.

We Don't Fire Anyone ...

Bobbi is director of OR services within a hospital that is very family-oriented in terms of patients and employees alike. She remembers the time she fired two nurses. The CEO found out and was very upset. She told Bobbi to reverse it. The unwritten rule was that no one was let go. Ever.

The new unwritten rule that surfaces when no one is let go is simply this—chaos. It encourages slacking—who has to excel at anything if there is lifetime tenure at work? Employee morale and productivity declines. It's like a disease that no one wants to talk about. She shared ...

> I knew the hospital "rule" that you did not fire someone. The real rule was that if you had a "bad" employee, you passed them on to another department and held your breath that it didn't backfire. When I attempted to do that, I was opposed by the other department manager, 'Thanks, but no thanks.' She didn't want them. I had no choice, their clinical skills were lacking and they were constantly disruptive within the unit. I terminated them.
>
> Now I am viewed as a cold-hearted bitch. In my professional opinion, they were a liability to me, as well as to the patients I serve.

Unwritten rules that say *"Do anything to retain personnel"* create problems. At times, the person who is retained will be an older employee, one who is close to retirement. She may be slowing down or her skills may be substandard and outmoded. Management believes that because she has been with the establishment for so long, she should be rewarded for her dedication and loyalty. Even to the risk of the patient.

In effect, management's unwritten rule is that it owes a lifetime job to every employee. When someone is not required to be competent, mediocrity becomes the norm. Bobbi had this problem in another instance, too. She continued ...

> I recently had another serious breach of discipline, due to negligence. I believed that another nurse should be terminated. We had done a case in surgery

where the instruments had not been sterilized.
When I questioned the nurse, she said that she knew
what she was supposed to do, but just didn't do it.
I found out that this was her normal practice yet
couldn't fire her. Her incompetence was passed on to
another department. Meanwhile, I hold my breath
that a patient doesn't get an infection or a lawsuit
doesn't hit.

   After I fired the first two nurses, there was a big
meeting. It was the first time anyone had ever been
fired from our department. Everyone was shocked. At
the meeting, the CEO said she hated getting up in the
morning and coming to work when the staff was not
happy. There was to be no more firings.

   Bobbi is correct. People may be unhappy or happy for a
variety of reasons, many of which may have nothing to do
with the workplace. Management is responsible for creating an environment that is safe, meets various standards,
delivers what it promises, and rewards competence. Guarantee happiness and lifelong employment with no strings
attached? Get real.

Identifying Your Unwritten Rules that Rule

Set aside 15 to 30 minutes over the next few days, and just
ponder scenarios in your workplace. Identify all the people you work and interact with—those in management or
supervisory positions and those in senior management,
including your CEO.

   Next, list the women and men you work with directly.
What about departments that you have to contact for maintenance of equipment or transportation needs? It's common for workplaces, especially hospitals, to represent
isolated silos—thinking that each stands alone and failing

to recognize that there is actually a great deal of integration and interaction.

As you identify the players in your workplace, describe their tasks, their personalities and the interactions you have with them. Ask yourself if they dress or speak in specific ways. Have the times when you had direct interaction with them been good, bad or indifferent? Is your workplace stimulating and energetic, or is it a drag for you to show up each day?

Write down your thoughts about the various individuals you work with. When images of your boss, supervisor or manager come to mind, are there any idiosyncrasies, mandates or dictums that also come to mind?

Now think about your colleagues and co-workers. Do you have rules regarding days off, break time, interactions or housekeeping? No matter how minor they seem, write down these rules, written or unwritten.

Brainstorm with a trusted colleague to expand your list, or at least collaborate on one. In staff meetings, if there is time set aside for comments and questions, you can involve others in identifying various unwritten rules.

Caution: If your manager or supervisor is not open to this idea, she may perceive your suggestion as threatening. If so, or if you are unsure about how your manager will respond, it might be better to approach your manager on a one-on-one basis. Since your objective is to identify unwritten rules and make life in your workplace more livable, try saying something like this: "Since I've been here, I have noticed a series of things that many do."

Now, identify some of those things. Everything you mention should be basically safe and nonthreatening. For example, it could be that everyone washes her own coffee cup, that certain coffee cups are not used, and that smoking is allowed only in specific areas.

Continue with a statement like this: "If I had known that these were unwritten rules, it would have been so much easier for me when I started here. Has anyone thought about putting together a notebook of other rules that our team goes by? When we add new employees or have temps and floaters, this list could give them a better understanding of what makes our unit tick."

It may make sense to be anonymous, for personal or even political reasons, and a suggestion box can be used to collect the "unwritten" rules. And some of the rules that emerge will be absurd, or sacred cows that everyone knows about and dislikes but are still untouchable. Violation of unwritten rules can drive others crazy. If you or someone else continually violates or ignores them, the workplace can become miserable for all.

JB's Keeper—

Before assuming that an unwritten rule really is untouchable or unchangeable, ask why? If you are not sure, ask someone you work with. Sometimes no one really knows why some of the unwitten rules are in place. Identify those rules and discuss them. If the group agrees, change them ... and tell others you have.

Have some fun identifying the unwritten rules of your workplace. Why not post an *Unwritten Rule of the Week* and have a good laugh with your co-workers? Give a prize for the silliest ... or even for uncovering one that may be costing your department moneys that could be allocated in another area.

The Players ...

Pit Bulls are loaded with unwritten rules, as are the Snakes, Skunks, Scorpions and Slugs of the workplace. But a key Pit Bull's unwritten rule is loyalty ... loyalty to the Pit Bull, her ideas and her ideals. If you cross the Pit Bull, you can become dinner. A savvy employee and manager will seek out the unwritten rules of the workplace, especially ones that are practiced by the Pit Bull.

Skunks operate under the unwritten rule that all change is bad. If you don't know that, you are likely to get sprayed with a variety of behaviors that aren't pleasant and very unwelcome. When a Skunk is identified within the workplace, it's smart to determine what rattles her, and the sooner the better. If a Skunk let's loose, the entire workplace is affected.

Snakes don't always share their unwritten rules with their friends, much less their co-workers. There is an assumption that you are supposed to intuitively know them, to be able to figure out what makes them tick and what the button pushers are that get them to rise up and move into a striking position. If a Snake is in your workplace, as with a Pit Bull and Scorpion, it's best to do all you can to figure out what her sacred cows are.

Scorpions share a lot of similarity with the Snakes. The one thing that will separate them from the Pit Bulls and Snakes is that even when the unwritten rules are known, they may not go along with them. Scorpions take care of themselves ... if they don't go along with or believe in the unwritten rules that others do, they don't care. If you point out their uncooperativeness, watch it, the stinger is lurking. It's their nature.

Slugs want to know the nuances and unwritten rules of the workplace. They want to be savvy about what they need to do and know to keep from screwing up. They don't want to be squashed from their ignorance, although not standing out is one of their personal unwritten rules.

Summing Up

Every workplace has written and unwritten rules, and they are different in each one. When you learn them, pass them on to others. Some are silly and harmless; some can be brutal and demeaning.

Don't get caught up in the "old games." The games that carried the unwritten rule that you had to always learn via the school of hard knocks. Some of those knocks can destroy one's confidence, even a career. Why play that game?

When you are oblivious to the unwritten rules, or when you don't speak out and pass them along, you set yourself up for a fall. You set others up, too, and everyone loses.

Keep in mind—it's not always the written rules (show up, do your job), it's the unwritten rules that can make or break you and your workplace.

7

Red Ink Behaviors ...
A Great Way
to Kiss-off a
Lot of Money

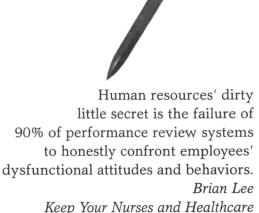

Human resources' dirty
little secret is the failure of
90% of performance review systems
to honestly confront employees'
dysfunctional attitudes and behaviors.
Brian Lee
Keep Your Nurses and Healthcare
Professionals for Life

*R*ed Ink Behaviors are the working manners, habits
and styles that can directly and negatively impact
the bottom line. I'm talking about money—lots of
it. Imagine these players in your workplace ...

- Mary is usually late for her shift two to three times
  a week.

- George spends a good part of his day talking about his latest extreme sports venture.
- Susan knows just about everything about a patient's family that anyone could imagine and she gleans the information in chatty phone calls with them.
- Cindy just can't seem to "remember" the way the doctor wants the procedure trays and room set up.
- Madison's motto is if it doesn't move, she doesn't have to either.
- Isabella reworks her paperwork so many times that you want to grab it and do it yourself.
- Martha doesn't respond to any issue until it moves into chaos.
- Nancy likes to give off bits and pieces of information, often withholding a critical piece.
- Laura gets in a real snit if you sit in her chair, use her pen or take your break before she gets to.
- Denise sounds like she's always talking in a foreign language, yet you know that she speaks the one that you are fluent in.
- Cathy cuts everyone off, never letting anyone get her point across.
- Sam leaves his co-workers and managers "guessing" what he really means.
- Jamie puts down every new idea that is presented at a staff meeting.
- Susie routinely "forgets" to give you your messages.
- Tom waits until the last minute to do any project, then gets others to drop whatever they are doing to assist him.
- Bertha ... Bertha is just ready to take the opposite point of view on anything—it doesn't matter what.

Does any of this sound familiar? Welcome to *Red Ink Behaviors*, a true curse of just about every workplace. Sometimes these behaviors are unconscious, people are truly not aware of what they are doing and what the impact is on others, their department and the organization. Most times, though, the creator is aware of the behaviors that irritate others and how they disrupt the "normal" flow of the workplace. In fact, they like to do what they know bugs someone and they really don't think about, much less care, if there is any financial consequence to their actions.

In either case, productivity suffers. With it, you lose money—it takes more time to complete tasks, meaning overtime or even the hiring of additional personnel.

Most organizations are not aware of the cost—what does a chatty phone call cost an employer? An employee who thrives in chaos, while those around him don't? Or, the withholding of information that could smooth a project's process or enable a co-worker to work more efficiently?

You don't need a PhD in Economics to know the answer ... it's simple—money. With few exceptions, there isn't a workplace, a department or organization that couldn't use more money.

Can a manager do a reasonable guesstimate of what bad behaviors cost? You bet. In fact, a manager must. As an employee, it's a smart thing to do as well.

When Red Ink Behavior is reined in, you will discover that less moneys go toward replacement and overtime costs. When groups reduce these behaviors, they discover that the need for overtime is reduced—in some cases, even personnel. That means money can be redirected to educational activities, or anything else that is desired. It becomes a win-win.

Although the health care sector will continue to grow in relation to overall national revenue and expenses, many facilities will still feel strapped for cash. Zillions of dollars come in, more zillions go out. A savvy manager needs to know all the avenues of disbursement—both in hard dollars and soft. Hard dollars you write checks for; soft dollars are stolen away from you in the form of lost time and inefficiencies that eat away at productivity.

The Domino Factor

The Pit Bulls, Skunks, Snakes, Scorpions and Slugs of the workplace all have ordinary names. Let's call them Bert and Bertha to cover both genders.

Imagine that Bert or Bertha has once again taken credit for the work that you have spent grueling hours on, to the extreme annoyance of your family and friends ... and you are a man. Or, that Bert or Bertha has once again taken credit for the work that you have spent grueling hours on, to the extreme annoyance of your family and friends . . . and you are a woman.

Same culprits, different recipient of the treatment. As a man, how are you most likely to react? As a woman, how are you most likely to react? Is there a difference in reactions and/or outcomes? Yes, there is.

JB's Keeper—

Every work environment has some such culprits—at times lurking in the corners in a stealth mode, at other times blatantly up front with their actions. Real time jerks and jerkettes who cost any employer big bucks ... and for the employee, possible lost productivity, maybe a ding on credibility, even a job.

The Difference

The challenge for women in the workplace (and for managers who manage them and co-workers) is that there is a difference in how men and women respond to the rotten players in their offices and work environments. Rotten players are riddled with *Red Ink Behaviors.* Men are more inclined to quickly evaluate what ole Bert and Bertha have done—they either confront the offender or decide that it's not worth their time and drop the situation.

Far fewer women take the man's approach—to directly confront or drop it. Women are more inclined to sidestep the conflict creator ... and then tell their workplace friends, co-workers, anybody else who's in listening range about what ole Bert and Bertha have pulled this time; they will share how upset they are and how it hurts or impacts them. Their listeners are sympathetic—empathetic. After all, they most likely have borne the brunt of bad behavior as well. It's the *Domino Factor*—everyone gets caught up in it.

The Cost to the Employer

Productivity, or the reduction of it, rears its head. So does turnover. This is where the male/female differences are measurable. Women report that when conflict and staboteurs lurk in their workplaces, it takes them two to four times as long to complete a task.

As an employer or manager, it's not difficult to figure out what the bad apples cost you and your department and organization. Get your calculator out. When good people leave—which is a direct result of keeping marginal employees like Bert and Bertha—you now must replace them, possibly paying finder's fees and/or signing bonuses. You may have to pay higher wages. You may even have to get more than one person to replace the good person who finally threw in the towel.

Here's an example. In a recent interview with a director in a hospital on the West Coast, I heard about a problem nurse—a woman whose behavior had led to five nurses quitting and going to a competing hospital within the past year. To replace the five nurses, she had to budget in excess of $400,000.

In addition, complaints bounced around the unit she worked in that work wasn't getting completed ... the *Domino Factor* was in motion. Many HR professionals are now factoring in as much as three times compensation to determine true replacement costs. In our survey, 46 percent of the respondents reported that when bad behavior was in play, their productivity nose-dived. It would not be surprising to find that that one marginal nurse had cost her unit in excess of $500,000 in lost productivity. Add that to the replacement cost of the estimated $400,000 and you have a tidy sum indeed!

Lesson Well Learned

Dennis has over 20 years of management experience. He's been a director of several units in medium size hospitals in the Rocky Mountain region. Dennis is the first to admit that he's a far better manager because of a team member who was so disruptive, literally contaminating the workplace environment, that he experienced a 100 percent turnover within the year. His words...

> One of my staff members was young, smart and someone who I felt had great potential. Whenever I initially approached her regarding the complaints that others had made directly to me about her behavior, she would react shocked. She wanted me to line up all the team members so she could confront each of them who said anything.

Early on, I ignored the complaints. I didn't appreciate what the power of her intimidation did to the rest of the team, which totaled 10 at the time. I failed to see the collateral consequences of her actions on others.

I began to document like crazy—in our system, there's a four-stage process before someone can be terminated. First there's a verbal warning, then a written, followed by a suspension and finally termination. During these stages, we do progress counseling.

Because I was in denial, it took me one and a half years to get through the process. I hadn't trusted the depth of what my staff was telling me. During this time, 100 percent of the team either transferred or quit. Several of them got physically ill if they saw on the schedule that they had to work with her. One even shared that her anxiety level was so high that at the end of the shift she couldn't sleep at night.

My guilt was horrible. My team wanted me to fix the problem. They came to me; initially, I told them that they just had to deal with her—I had no understanding of how her behaviors and actions really affected them. Finally, I knew I had to. I went to HR during the progressive counseling stage and told the director that my goal was to get enough documented evidence that she could and would be let go.

Dennis came away with a valuable lesson—a lesson that he uses within his own departments and with his managers today. He now knows that you can't ignore complaints. They only fester and domino. Nipping things in the bud is critical, before anything can escalate. As he adds ...

One of my key takeaways was that you have to get comfortable having uncomfortable conversations with disruptive team members. One of the primary roles of a manager is to protect the team and the environment they work in. I failed the first time around and I'm a much better manager because of the chaos and destruction she created. It's an example I share often of *what not to do*.

When employees report that they are experiencing physical and emotional reactions to someone's bad behavior a major warning is being sounded to management; management must heed it. The cost of replacing 10 people is in the hundreds of thousands of dollars. None of these factors should be taken lightly.

The splintering of Dennis' team took a physical, emotional and financial toll on everyone.

What to Do

As a manager, you need to tune in to the different styles of handling conflict. You need to acknowledge that it exists, determine its roots and work on resolution. If you don't, it grows. No one needs a PhD to determine that.

Not all conflict is bad—some good changes come about because resolution is finally forced. But, when it grows, dominoes and is unresolved, your bottom line is hit and red ink flows—productivity dives, team morale plummets, turnover increases—who wants to work in that kind of environment?

As an employee, it's important to look in the mirror and determine how you handle conflict. Do you identify the source, get your facts, confront the problem and work for resolution? Or, do you bite your tongue, only to share it with others (never the conflict-creator) or act on it at a later time in a revenge mode?

Who Are the Pissy People?

Fifty percent now report that they have left jobs because of abusive and subversive behaviors and 51 percent said that they wouldn't come back even if the jerk or jerkette was terminated. Can you head off abusers and are there tell-tale signs of disruptive and unproductive behavior? Yes.

Thousands of managers and employees who complain and grumble about staff and co-workers offered their input. Many openly said that they are aware of employees who have quit and gone to work somewhere else. The primary reasons? Their workplace environment is the pits—it's toxic. Poor and abrasive managers or bullying and non-collaborative co-workers top the list.

It's the Toxic Workplace Syndrome, a chronic disorder that costs money—included could be overtime pay, replacement costs including signing bonuses, orientation, lower productivity because of training for the new hire, and possible moving reimbursements.

So, open your eyes and ears. Ask yourself—

Is Red Ink Behavior in Your Midst?

1. If there is overtime, is it excessive, and why is it needed?
2. Is productivity lower in your department or office than in others that are similar?
3. Is work just not getting done?
4. Are you getting complaints or hearing others continually complain about others or co-workers?
5. Is there grumbling, complaining or general chit-chat where work literally shuts down any type of productivity when the latest "issue" is chewed over—the Domino Factor?

6. Is there someone who everyone avoids dealing with?
7. Are deadlines repeatedly missed?
8. Is absenteeism high?
9. Is there a high level of tardiness (coming to work as well as returning from breaks)?
10. Is there someone who always seems to find the negative in whatever is being proposed or suggested?
11. Do people ask to transfer to another department or quit—and tell the exit interviewer the reason they are leaving is for a "better" opportunity or being closer to home?
12. Do you ever feel that your workplace is the pits?

A yes to any of the above means you need to probe. Money is going down the drain.

Red Ink Behaviors in the Midst

Over 20 years ago I lived in the heart of Silicon Valley, the land of Apple Computer, Hewlett Packard and now Google. It was where the seeding of my first book on women and sabotage in the workplace—*Woman to Woman: From Sabotage to Support* started. One of the leadership stars of the valley was Jean Hollands, the CEO of the Growth & Leadership Center in Mountain View, California. She was the one who coined the phrase *Red Ink Behaviors*. Since that time, I've continued to add to it.

Pinpoint areas that you can identify with both staff and administration. Which ones, and combinations, could be lethal for your department or office?

- Anger—always has a chip on the shoulder, has a short fuse in dealing with situations or seems hostile

- Arrogance—is better than anyone and/or above it all
- Attacks—blows up at the slightest situation, often turning a very small mole hill into a mountain
- Authenticity—doesn't walk their talk or talk their walk
- Awareness—is clueless to how their behavior impacts others
- Backstabbing—friendly to one's face, but lethal when they are gone
- Barriers—is evasive and keeps others at bay
- Bullying—belittles and cuts others down
- Collaboration—cooperation isn't in their vocabulary
- Communication—doesn't
- Complains—takes the opposing side in most discussions
- Confidence—lacks self-esteem and confidence and doing/completing projects and tasks
- Conflict—ignites and adds to it
- Controlling—almost impossible not to meddle or be involved
- Covertness—routinely displays activities and behavior in a shadow format or behind the scenes
- Credit—claims accomplishments of others as well as discounts their contributions
- Criticizes—without any sensitivity to others
- Defensive—has a chip on their shoulder and appears that they are ready to attack
- Domino Factor—doesn't confront and shares everything with everyone, over and over
- Empathy—does not demonstrate concern or care for co-workers
- Feedback—reacts negatively to others giving it
- Fire hoses—routinely negates new ideas and creativity generated by others

- Flexibility—resists change and doesn't adapt well to procedural changes
- Front-stabbing—blatantly undermines in front of all, including victim
- Gossip—is a messenger of personal news about co-workers
- High Maintenance—managers spend lots of time dealing, talking, thinking about
- Humor—lacks a sense of one
- Inflames—adds fuel to difficult situations
- Inspiration—incapable of encouraging and cheering others on
- Isolates—keeps others out of the information loop
- Listening—is selective, only hearing what appeals to them
- Mentoring—doesn't receive or give; difficulty creating coaching relationships
- Perspective—doesn't read or interpret others well
- Power—routinely discounts or ignores another's power
- Priority—unable to distinguish what's important, and what's not
- Proactive—doesn't initiate things, waits to react
- Procrastinates—waits until the last minute to do anything
- Reactionary—rarely is proactive; waits for something to happen
- Realigns—workplace friendships and relationships don't stick
- Reality Check—doesn't check back with others, often stubborn in beliefs and not open to others' viewpoints and opinions
- Reluctant—rarely reaches out to assist, teach, coach, or to share info

- Repairability—can't mend difficult situations
- Resists—routinely digs in heels to doing things their way
- Rigid—resists all, wants to keep the status quo
- Sabotage—undermines others' activities; could be intentional or unintentional
- Sarcastic—cuts others down and creates distrust
- Stabotage—intentionally undermines others' activities
- Stress—a stress creator and carrier
- Team Player—lacks both social and workplace skills to be involved as a member
- Tolerance—non-accepting of others
- Trust—lacks faith in others as well as the ability to create confidence in and from them
- Uncooperative—isn't a team player, isolated and cares little about others or getting something done in a timely manner
- Un-empowered—feels hopeless and out of control
- Vision—has little and rarely thinks beyond today; lacks the big picture
- Withholds Information—uses as a power play

What Red Ink Behavior Is in Your Workplace?

At this point, it's your turn. I opened this chapter with a few behaviors and styles that could constitute *Red Ink Behavior*—from working with a chaos creator, tardiness, withholding information, being cynical and cryptic in communicating to having too many chatty phone calls. Add to the list below things that you are aware of that are costing you (and your department) time and money. And, look in the mirror: are you the creator of any?

Who Creates It?	What Is It?	How Much Is the Cost?
_____	_____	_____
_____	_____	_____
_____	_____	_____
_____	_____	_____

Of the ones you have listed above, which ones do you feel are the most costly? Why?

Next up is crunching the numbers. What is this costing you?

If you are a *manager*, everyone who works for you gets paid. Every department has some percentage of turnover—some high, some low. Turnover comes from a variety of areas. Write below the number of employees in your department, the average annual turnover and the average moneys you are paying. Don't forget overtime, benefits and any bonuses.

Department _____
Number of Employees _____
Average Annual Compensation _____
Annual Turnover # _____
Percent of Turnover to the # of Employees _____
Replacement Costs at 100% _____
Replacement Costs at 150% _____
Replacement Costs at 300% _____

If you are an *employee*, you get paid as others do. You may not know what your co-workers get, although most employees are aware of hourly ranges—e.g., $18 to $36 an hour. For annual compensation, double the hourly rate and multiply by 1000—$36,000 to $72,000. Don't forget overtime and benefits.

   Interesting, employees rarely consider benefits—from the employer contribution to Social Security, retirement accounts, education grants, vacation, personal time off and the like—as part of compensation. It is.

   Let's say you work either in a department with 12 or 47 employees and two leave during the year, you have the turnover number. Divide the number who left by the total number of a full department. If two left the department of 12, then it's 2 divided by 12 = 16.7%; or if 2 left the department of 47, then divide 2 by 47 = 4.3%

   Feeling a tad baffled? Let me work one through for you. Let's say you manage or work in the Women's & Children's Services and there are 152 nurses with an average income of $72,000 (that's $36 an hour). During the past year, 29 have left for a variety of reasons. Your numbers look like this—

Department	Women's & Children's Services
Number of Employees	152
Average Annual Compensation	$72,000
Annual Turnover #	29
Turnover %	29 /152 = 19%
Replacement @100%	$ 72,000 x 29 = $2,088,000
Replacement @150%	$108,000 x 29 = $3,132,000
Replacement @300%	$216,000 x 29 = $6,264,000

The Spill-Over Factor

In our survey, 52 percent reported that they had to "cover" for others' incompetencies. They add that it *takes two to four times* as long to complete tasks when conflict creators, staboteurs are in action. The same goes for those who create *Red Ink Behavior*—many of these behaviors crossover to outright stabotage.

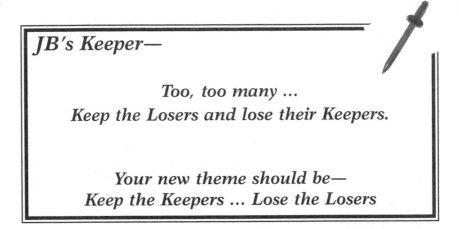

JB's Keeper—

Too, too many ...
Keep the Losers and lose their Keepers.

Your new theme should be—
Keep the Keepers ... Lose the Losers

How much time, energy and money are you willing to kiss-off by refusing to deal with the bad behaviors of your workplace?

The Players ...

Pit Bulls blast out their *Red Ink Behaviors* and don't give a twit for whom or what they use them on. Pit Bulls embrace conflict, the more, the better. With their blunt and aggressive style, their guiding behaviors become anger, stabotage, blowing up and control. Being a team player isn't a key factor for them ... being outspoken, pushy and in charge is their preference.

Skunks are visible critters, usually hyping up their behaviors when they are fearful. They are more inclined to become inflamed when change, uncertainty and high levels of stress are in play. Skunks act out initially in a covert manner until their posturing and behavior surfaces and can no longer be disguised.

Snakes are reactionary. When they are threatened, they immediately move into position to strike back. Using their tongues, their body language tells you to keep away, that they've created a barrier to block progress for the team, and you.

Scorpions also are masters at being covert. They lack most team-playing skills and have no desire to learn them or for that matter, learn anything beyond what they need to know to keep them at the status quo. They usually like to mind their own business until something strikes their fancy or riles them. They are master backstabbers and when their stingers strike, you may wonder where did that come from, there had been no clue.

Slugs cover a variety of *Red Ink Behaviors*. They're not bullies, but they are masters at whining and complaining; of not reaching out and learning new things. Slugs are uninspiring. The only type of mentoring they would engage in is that of negative mentoring—demonstrating the bad habits that they've honed to just get by. The productivity of a slug, is, well, like a slug. Zip gets done.

Summing Up ...

Red Ink Behaviors are too often accepted in the workplace as simply "Well, that's the way she is ... he is..." Until the true cost of the dominoing factors of pissy, arrogant, rude, fire-hosing and any of the other behaviors identified in this chapter are acknowledged, workplaces will lose money and people. In the end, it's a never-ending story.

8

Communicate, Communicate, Communicate ... It's About **You**

The greatest problem
in communication is the illusion
that it has taken place ...
George Bernard Shaw, playwrite

One of the most powerful tools you will acquire is communicating: being able to speak loudly and clearly so that what you meant to convey is understood, and having the verbal savvy to articulate your words in the right context. *When dealing with and confronting a staboteur or conflict creator, communicating effectively is essential.*

For *Seinfeld* watchers, one of the classic episodes starts in the foursome's favorite haunt, Monk's Restaurant. Jerry, Elaine, Kramer and his girlfriend of the month are at their regular table. Kramer gets up to make a phone call. Both

Jerry and Elaine attempt to engage the woman in conversation to no avail. The best they can get from her is a few mumbles and whispers every time they ask her a question. In desperation, the both nod their heads and verbally go along with whatever she is whispering—after all, they don't want to be impolite to their pal's latest squeeze.

The next morning, Jerry is slated to be on the *Today* show with Bryant Gumbel interviewing him. When he arrives at the studio, he is escorted to the Green Room, he finds an ironing board and Kramer's mumbling maven ironing a ridiculous looking shirt for Jerry to wear. Jerry is ticked and can't believe that he's been duped.

How did Jerry get in this pickle? Quite simply—it's miscommunication. Whenever I do a survey on workplace issues and concerns, communication snafus head the list. Communication—wrong, missed, nil or none—are common complaints in today's workplace. It doesn't matter if they are scripted as on TV or in real life. Miscommunications happen, whether you are speaking or listening.

> **Communicating means to translate your message into a clear, concise statement or concept that the receiver understands.**

Sounds fairly simple, and at most times, harmless. Why then, do most people do such a miserable job at it?

Although the great majority of people in the United States speak English, they too often fail to understand that their jargon, mannerisms, jokes, stories—whatever ways and means they use to communicate—is ineffective. Why? Even though we speak a common language, it is no guarantee that we understand it the same way.

My jargon for a certain occurrence can be totally different from yours. If I use my style, and you don't fully understand what I really mean—I have failed in my attempt to communicate with you.

> **Those who lack communication skills are often labeled less confident, less attractive, and less qualified to do a job.**

There are four steps to being an effective communicator. Those steps have parts for both the speaker and the receiver. Included are:

If you are the speaker—
1. Speak loudly enough to enable the listener to hear whatever your message is.
2. Speak clearly so that the listener understands what you mean.
3. Use terms and words that will be of interest to the listener. When possible, use their jargon, their word phrases, and examples that can be easily identified and related to.
4. Be specific, call for action. Don't just fill the air with words; be prepared to ask for help, deliver a plan, and so on.

If you are the listener—
1. Hear the message generated by the speaker in an unobstructed manner. Outside noise and interference (phones ringing, using e-mail, others interrupting, etc.) lead to hit and miss hearing. You lose.

2. Understand what the message is. If you are unclear or not sure exactly what is being said, it's your responsibility to ask for clarity from the speaker. Or, you lose again.

3. Appreciate the fact that the speaker is attempting to convey his or her message in a manner that can be absorbed. This doesn't mean it has to be agreed with, but merely that you understand that the message is coming across in a communication style and language that you understand.

4. You have the responsibility to participate in the request of the speaker. You may agree or disagree with what is called for in the action request, but you need to respond, to act on it.

The bottom line in communicating is knowing and understanding that most communication are non-verbal. Words are just a portion of the communication package—gestures, tones and body language are critical. As the speaker, the initiator of the communication process, it is your responsibility to make sure your listener understands your meaning and intent. As a listener, it is your responsibility to receive, comprehend and act on the message.

Jerry learned his lesson in The Puffy Shirt episode. Whose fault was it? Primarily, his. He didn't say, "Whoa, I can't hear you—speak up." Or, "I don't understand what you are saying, please repeat it ... or restate it." Was he manipulated? Of course he was. But, he chose to go along with it and then is shocked to find out that by nodding affirmatively, even though he didn't understand her, he had agreed to wear the absurd shirt on national TV.

Speaking, listening. Listening, speaking. It doesn't sound too complicated, yet millions fail everyday. Don't you.

JB's Keeper—

*Most health care professionals are behind
the times. While the great majority of
workplaces and employees are fairly
computer and Internet savvy, health care
professionals comes in a distant second.
Ironically, when I ask audience attendees
at health care conferences if they are
proficient with personal computers and
the workings of the Internet, fewer than
20 percent respond that they are.*

*Get over your technophobia. It's time
to dust off the keyboard. A whole new world
opens up, one that every health care provider
should have some familiarity with.*

*Don't know where to start? Here's an idea ...
hire an eight year old. These kids are incredible
in getting you started on the basics ... and
they still like us adults (as opposed to a lot
of teens who've forgotten how to dialogue
once their hormones kick in).*

It's the Nonverbals

In the summer of 2007, the Colorado Rockies baseball team secured its league pennant. For the first time in its history, the team played in the World Series. Denver, and most of Colorado, went baseball crazy. The Rockies' colors, purple and black, were everywhere the eye can see. I know ... I live here.

Although the Rockies lost to the Red Sox in the Series, the team was still the talk of the town. How did it, having been in the cellar so long, rise to the top? And how did the team do it? Without going into a diatribe about talent and money and being in the right place at the right time, I'll venture to say communicating effectively was part of their formula.

The great majority of communicating is below the radar. "It's not what you say—it's how you say it" is a phrase for our times. All you have to do is watch the nonverbal signals from coach to player and player to player to know that there's another language that you and I don't know. Sure, verbal is critical, but so is the nonverbal.

Today's workplace is no different. It requires, demands, expert communication. Take listening. Are there differences between men and women?

My experience says yes. In the 25 years I've been researching and writing about workplace behaviors, I've found that women usually pay more attention, particularly to the nonverbal side of communication, than men do—that is, the expressions that face, gestures and body positioning reveal.

According to communication experts, of all the elements within our communication repertoire (e.g., writing, speaking, listening), we spend the greatest single percentage of our communication time listening—approximately 45 percent.

Listening is using your ears and eyes, but what the eyes can tell you can often put you at the head of the class. The mouth may say one thing, but the body may say something totally different. If you fail to listen accurately, you most likely have experienced the greatest single problem in communication. Listening is critical.

Let's fast forward to today's workplace. I love the technology. When I'm in my office, my multitasking skills are in full swing. All e-mail programs are open, phones (land and cell) are in use and I communicate—in person and electronically— with staff. If I feel it's important, I go to the other person's office so I can see them as we interact.

Why?—simply this: I hear more.

Data that is often quoted by trainers in communication was first introduced by Albert Mehrabian, a professor at UCLA in California. Its focus is on first impressions— what comes across in those first few seconds when first encountering someone—it can be someone you know or don't know.

Let's do the math. Fifty-five percent of what's communicated in that first impression is visual. What the person is wearing, colors, styles, accessories, body position, body movement, facial and hand expressions, etc., are taken in.

Picture this: think about the last time you saw someone who looked like she was a walking billboard for the metal piercing industry, someone whose jeans were barely hanging around their hips, someone who has crossed her arms or even turned her back, or someone whose hair is fuchsia. Haven't you already come to some conclusions about what that person is about without hearing one word?

The tone that the voice generates accounts for another 38 percent. When I mention this in my speeches, I always use the example of the "teen tone"—you know, the one that tells the adult (usually the parent) that he or she is basically dull and stupid (I had three teens—I know this one well!). It's sometimes accompanied with a roll of the eyes. The tone used in communicating tells reams about the speaker.

So, that leaves a mere 7 percent open to the actual words of what is said.

Remember, this is the first go around when you meet someone ... not the long-term interaction. After the "warm-up," those percentages shift. Too many professional speakers, trainers and consultants continue to cite Mehrabian's work as the "way we communicate... always." Wrong, it's only the first impression. Visual intake is often tops with many, but other factors come into play.

JB's Keeper—

Use common words to say or convey uncommon ideas, situations or events.

What Is Seen Is What You Say ...

Have you ever been at a function, be it with a dozen or many, many more, and you've experienced one of those brain-dead things ... you've forgotten the name of someone you were just introduced to?

You painstakingly try to remember the guy's name, hoping that someone will come along and call him by his name and bail you out. You hesitate to ask again, truth-be-told, you don't want him to think that you weren't listening when you were initially introduced. No one comes to your rescue.

What gives? *Are* you brain-dead? You can recall the tie, the color, even the knot, just no name. Are you displaying early signs of dementia setting in?

Nope, in fact, you are normal. Most people size up someone in that first meeting based on the visual take—body language, facial, hand and feet gestures/positioning, what colors, clothing and accessories are worn—you name it, anything that the eye can take in registers on the imprint scale. The simple fact is that you just didn't hear the name; you had other things on your mind.

In the Sixties, John F. Kennedy debated Richard Nixon in the first televised presidential debate. If you watched on TV, Kennedy won; if you listened on the radio, Nixon won. The deal breaker—it was the five o'clock shadow along with no makeup that the camera displayed to the viewing public. They didn't like it.

When it comes to the first impression, the eyes have it. What's important to you is to know and understand that your body language and how you visually present yourself could be a deal breaker. Today's best leaders and communicators know that a commanding visual presence says competence and confidence.

When I was a kid, no one had a TV in every room. Most families could own only one, so that whatever was viewed would be more of the family-fare variety. The variety show was popular. Some starred well-known names like Bob Newhart, Dean Martin, Ed Sullivan, Dinah Shore and the like. They would frequently have guests, often musically oriented.

A mainstay was entertainer Victor Borge, one of the outrageously funny masters of communication. His reading of a text, any text, coupled with his sound effects for every dot, comma, colon, semi-colon, question mark, exclamation mark and quote mark he came to were hilarious. It was also dead on.

He added his facial expressions and used his hands to add to the shapes of the various marks. No one forgot his performance. The viewer/audience was thoroughly entertained and remembered what he was reading to boot.

So it goes with your own interviews and performance evaluations. Not that you have to do a Victor Borge, but it's career-smart to understand the language of nonverbal communication.

Let's start with some of the Don'ts" ...

- Don't put your hands in your pockets or keep them "stuck" by your side ... it may be read that you are insecure.
- Don't slouch in a chair ... it says that you are not interested, even lazy.
- Don't slump when you stand ... it can be read that you aren't paying attention or don't care.
- Don't wear just anything ... if it's a wrong fit, style, color, it says you didn't take the time to prepare.
- Don't wear colors that dull your skin tones ... the wrong color can actually make you look sick.
- Don't break eye contact ... when you break away, it can feign a non-interest.

The "Do" List is critical ...

- Do lean forward if sitting ... it shows some interest and enthusiasm.
- Do pay attention to your hands and nails... are they clean, manicured—hands speak volumes.

- Do be animated ... use your hands and your facial expressions to accent key points.
- Do pay attention to your arms and legs ... if they are uncrossed, it says that "I'm not blocking you out..."
- Do keep eye contact ... it says I'm listening and connecting.
- Do wear colors and styles that are flattering ... this goes for women and men alike.
- Do communicate, in writing, after the interview... a hand-written thank you note for the interview is just smart and can put you on the short list for follow-up.

Masters of communication know that a job interview or evaluation can be made before one word is spoken. It happens with what you physically present yourself as, along with what comes out of your mouth and how you bring the two together.

Any sign of insincerity, disinterest or disrespect will get you out the door as quickly as a blatant overture that you don't give a twit.

By paying attention to what others see, you will discover that they will pay attention to the words you use and say.

Your body language says more about you than thousands of words. You want to be seen as an informed, responsible and savvy person. Are you?

Technology Speaks . . . Do You Hear?

Technology is wonderful—the advances within the health care community are incredible. Imagine if you have to have open-heart surgery, an organ transplant or a dental implant using the techniques that were common even 15 years ago. I doubt that you would be at the head of the line for choosing to do it the "old" way.

The way we communicate has also been impacted by technology, too. Information can be distributed the old fashion way—by mouth, letter, memo, phone—and then there's the new way, the Internet and e-mail. The great majority of households have Internet access; over 90 percent of businesses and organizations use it; and the great majority of patients use it.

The Internet is a fountain of information (most terrific, some rumored, some wrong and definitely a lot of useless junk)—and is a source that is routinely used to gather information about anything related to an illness or procedure, or even information about a related organization, association or career. Presto—it's all there with a few strokes on the keyboard.

It's not uncommon for a patient to arrive at a doctor's bringing a printout of everything related to his or her disease in a file. It's also not uncommon for the same patient to be more current about what's going on and recommended treatments than the health care providers are. Many medical and dental practices are setting up e-mail hours to communicate online with their patients. Hospitals are sure to follow. Clear and quick communication delivered via e-mail can certainly reduce conflicts with patient and provider.

Communicating Should Be the First Language

Susan is a radiology nurse. There are ten others in the department besides her; three who speak a foreign language. She reports,

When we have department meetings, I feel that the differences in language and understanding create barriers. More times than not, I feel my concerns and the things that I would like to see done are never heard. I don't believe the others are tuned in to the communication differences when the native English-speaking members don't fully understand the others' native tongues, or their customs.

Sometimes I wonder if it's on purpose.

It's not uncommon to hear a phrase such as "I was zinged" or "I was zapped" by someone. Staboteurs are quite good at it. Typically the issue isn't non-communication, but rather misconstrued communication.

Melanie is a nurse manager in a large hospital. Seven other managers work in her department, each reporting to the same director. She says,

It is routine for one of the managers to gather a bag-load of minor situations and heap them on the table at our monthly meetings. From someone who was late 10 minutes to another who didn't chart in a timely manner. Most are minor. Everything was unloaded at once and the director began to believe that we couldn't handle anything on our floors and shifts.

It wasn't uncommon for me and the other nurse manager to zap her back with a laundry list of problems. It got out of control.

Finally, several of us told her that it would be much more helpful to resolve whatever the problem is by bringing it to us immediately, or at least by the next day, when it involves another shift. Why hold it off for several weeks and put us on the spot as if we were incompetent?

Initially, she denied not dealing with issues as they occurred. But we were ready—we cited various examples of when, where and what she did. We all finally agreed that we did have a communication problem and agreed to keep talking to try to resolve it.

JB's Keeper—

If minor issues of the workplace are not dealt with, they become erupting volcanoes.

When one person tosses a zinger at another, whether it is a staff employee or someone in management, it leaves a bad taste.
The recipient is ticked. A common reaction is to verbally toss something back. The cycle continues, and if not nipped early on, will infest the workplace, turning it toxic. Morale and cooperation plummet.

Apologizing, Hedging & Qualifying

A factor that appears to be a greater drawback for women than for men is the use of *polite* speech. On one side, it shows a high regard and respect for another. That's not bad. Some cultures covet this behavior. But there are times when too polite speech lacks the necessary assertiveness.

In almost every book on communication, there is mention of women's use of tag questions and qualifiers. Whether women use them more than men is not clear. There is an ongoing debate. The important fact is for you to be aware if you are using speech mannerisms that can be misinterpreted. Typical tag questions include:

"This needs to be completed by four o'clock. Is that OK with you?"

"We need to be at the meeting at 10 AM tomorrow. Is that a problem for you?"

Where the first sentence is declarative, the second sentence—the *tag*—can be interpreted as a window for choice. The receiver of the remark may say, "No, it's not OK with me." "Yes, it's a problem."

Other factors of nonassertive speech patterns that can get you into trouble include the use of *qualifiers*. Qualifiers are often interpreted as a form of discounting what is being said. Qualifiers are hedges—words or phrases that make you sound uncertain ...

"You know," "Sorta," "I guess," "I suppose,""Like..."

When you are uncertain, qualifiers are perfectly legitimate. But as fillers or hedges, they lessen your power when communicating with another. Examples of beginning-sentence phrases are:

"I'm not sure that this is a good idea, but..."

"You may think this is dumb (stupid, silly, idiotic), but ..."

Women also get into trouble when they use too many adverbs or adjectives. The result is that their speech is sometimes trivialized. Such as:

"It's so lovely and wonderful to be here today.

"I think this is so very wonderful, exciting, and fabulous. I know it's going to be beyond belief."

Sometimes, women feel inhibited to ask for something boldly. So as not to appear so bold, we commonly soften a statement. Let's say you want to go to lunch. Instead of saying, "Let's go to lunch" to a co-worker, you might say,

"Gosh, I'm famished, and I've been so busy ... would you like ... oh, you're probably really busy too, and don't have time to take a break ... or do you think you'd like to get a bite to eat with me??????"

Because many women are process-oriented in their relationships, they are that way with answers and explanations as well. When someone asks you something, it's not uncommon to tell in detail the reasons why you arrived at your answer. Some people love to hear all the details; others don't. They'd rather you focus on the bottom-line impact.

JB's Keeper—

Women need to learn goal-oriented language to relate their messages more effectively. Sometimes, being blunt creates the best, and quickest, results. Do it.

When people apologize, it is usually an expression of regret at having done something wrong to another. Unfortunately, women are harder on and more judgmental about themselves when it comes to accepting or taking on blame. Men tend to apologize only when it is expected or when it can't be avoided. In fact, sometimes men never say, "I'm sorry." Instead, they make another statement with the "I'm sorry" implied, as in, "I screwed up."

One of the reasons men avoid apologizing is that it tends to put them in an inferior position. Since women are often people pleasers, being apologetic doesn't make them feel put down. According to Deborah Tannen, PhD and author of *You Just Don't Understand* ...

> There are many ways that women talk that make sense and are effective in conversation with other women. When in conversation with men, they appear powerless and self-deprecating. One such pattern is that women seem to apologize all the time.

One thing to keep in mind is that it is not necessary to apologize in a situation over which you have no control. If a land mine is exposed (or explodes), it's sufficient to state whatever the problem is (with no apologies), followed by recommended solutions to fix it.

What Tannen implies is that when the issue is between women, it's OK to apologize; in fact, it can be advantageous in creating a bond and even encouraging intimacy. For men, though, apologizing may be construed as a weakness.

Another common speech faux pas is inviting disagreement. When you have a strong opinion about a situation, or you require someone's participation, it doesn't make sense to preface your statement or request with a disclaimer ...

"I may have goofed, but..."

"This probably won't go over well, but..."

Not only do such statements lessen your speech and presence power, they also invite your listeners to move into a defensive posture, and disagree with you before you have a chance even to make a statement. *Staboteurs who are being confronted look for windows to disagree or counter what you are attempting to get across.* Being friendly can do wonders in the right place at the right time, but it also can be a distraction. Don't chitchat excessively.

Years ago, John Gray wrote the best seller *Men Are from Mars and Women Are from Venus.* For book titles, it gets an A+. But to run your life by it, adjust your thinking. I save many of the cards that people have sent me over the years. One of my favorites was a postcard that said: *Men are from Earth. Women are from Earth. Deal with it.*

JB's Keeper—

"Deal with it" is the perfect and right-on advice for today. It's long overdue in looking beyond the Mars/Venus phenomenon ... the simple fact is that it's just not men and women who might communicate a tad differently ... it's also the culture, generation and age variances that add to the pie of life. Learn about them, understand them ... deal with them.

What to Avoid When the Communication Cop Isn't There

Unassertive-type mannerisms can get everyone in trouble. It's not unusual for a woman to maintain constant eye contact with the person she is talking to. That's the good news; don't avoid doing this. Good eye contact is a communication gesture that should be mastered early on by both genders. With it, you are more likely to be taken seriously.

For a man, it's quite common to embrace a "darting" approach ... hopping around with the eyes, rarely connecting with the person being talked to. The result is that your remarks can easily be interpreted as meaning you're not serious, or you're nervous. A subtle message can be sent that your concern, opinion or statement is not important. When you don't make eye contact with a staboteur you are attempting to confront, you can signal fear or submissiveness, or even invite interruption.

In addition to using speech patterns that are unassertive, pay attention to inappropriate smiling and other gestures. Women are far more likely to smile inappropriately, especially during times of conflict, than are men. Both men and women will interpret a smile during a stressful or conflicting time to mean that all is OK, you're OK, and the issue is not as big a deal as you feel it is.

Laughing and giggling sometimes happens when one is nervous. But when stress or pain is present, it's not a fit. One of the best things that a woman can do is learn to keep a straight face, especially when it comes to dealing with a staboteur. Your goal is to get your point across—that the behavior directed toward you (or another) is not OK.

Normally, when listeners nod their head up and down, most people assume that they agree with the speaker. Not necessarily so. Women tend to nod their heads during a conversation more so than do men—even when they don't agree with or understand what's being said. It's more a mannerism of taking information in.

Warding Off Staboteurs in Your Midst

Consider the classic movie *Gone with the Wind.* In it, Scarlett O'Hara displayed every stereotypical female tendency imaginable. At times, she was soft and cute. She could be coy and manipulative. And she could run over anyone as if she were Attila the Hun.

Miss Scarlett was as competitive as any man that she encountered. In fact, one of her key attractions to Rhett the hunk was that she was like him in so many ways!

She was assertive, innovative, creative, pushy and at times downright revengeful in order to get what she wanted—just as some of the men were. Rhett knew—it takes one to know one.

In other words, the lovely Miss Scarlett did what she had to do to get what she wanted. Yawn. The men were no different.

When you were a kid, you probably heard an adult (most likely Mom) say, "Be patient, Honey, your turn will come." Patience wasn't in Scarlett's vocabulary. Plotting, planning and conniving were her modus operandi. She didn't believe that her turn would come. Rather, if she was going to get what she wanted, she had to create the path to get there and make it her turn. She took it. So should you.

The people that you communicate with, whether it's a friendly and non-adversarial situation, or it's a confronting and adversarial one, will communicate with and to you in different styles.

- Some are direct in their communication—the bottom liners, want minimal information. Don't waste their time, just get to the point.
- Some are data gatherers—the more information they get, the better; so pile it on.
- Some react and speak intuitively and emotionally— they follow their gut reactions and hunches, even sensing what you might want to say before you open your mouth.
- Some are more interested in maintaining peace and harmony—they never raise their voices and try to get all sides heard and are patient until everyone has their voice heard.
- Some communicate over multiple channels—the ultimate multi-taskers. They jump around and have difficulty focusing on any one topic or person at a time ... and sometimes because they jump around so much, they only hear bits and pieces ... which can lead to more miscommunication.
- Some "speak" your native tongue, but they seem to speak in a foreign language or use foreign devices ... if you have a teen or college kid in your household, think text messaging and teen's unique jargon.
- Some are silent, almost passive—they take it in, but have difficulty articulating what they want or what their concerns are. You may assume that they "get" what you said. Don't.

Your ability to speak up and out is the basis of clear and honest communication between you and another. Most communication and behaviors fall into four categories: assertive, passive/submissive (nonassertive), confusing and aggressive. Aggressive behaviors can be divided into direct and indirect.

JB's Keeper—

***If you demonstrate confidence and respect
for yourself, being assertive is rarely difficult.***

Being a doormat is not a position to be in. When you
have low confidence and feel that your opinions or beliefs
are of little or no value, you often feel like a doormat. You
become "invisible." If you appear or act with low confidence or passiveness, your behavior is easily interpreted
as being a "wimp." You are fair game for the staboteurs
and conflict creators of the world.

For effective and assertive communication to change a
behavior or an outcome, these need to be included:

- A nonjudgmental description of what you want
  changed.
- A disclosure of how you feel.
- A description of how the behavior was interpreted.
- A clear description of the impact effect of the other
  person's behavior on you.
- A description of what behavior you desire.
- A question that requires a "buy-in" that they will
  commit.
- A consequence if the behavior doesn't change.

When you speak clearly and succinctly, you are far
more likely to gain the respect and trust of others. You are
also less likely to be a target of a staboteur and the critters
of the workplace.

If a staboteur does bring you into her sights, you have the tools to clearly articulate what you expect in the future. But that's not a 100 percent guarantee; there are always those who will respond to your assertiveness with put-downs or other demands.

You have a decision to make. Are there more positives to outweigh the negativity that you are encountering? Or is this place, this situation the pits? The pits requires an exit ... the sooner, the better.

When you are communicating a problem, make sure you communicate the real issue and the factors within the problem, and make sure you communicate to the right person. If you are communicating a specific issue that you desire to be changed, make sure you communicate it to the person who has the capability of making the changes.

Never waste your time grumbling to someone who can't do anything but offer a shoulder of empathy. Find out who the decision maker is and don't take a "no" from someone who can't tell you "yes."

Depending on the degree of conflict or sabotage you are dealing with, the identified staboteur is the person to be confronted and communicated with.

Delete the Silence Trap

Communicating effectively was at the top of the survey respondents' list in dealing with workplace issues. To be believable in any work environment, the silence trap of not dealing directly with an issue (versus the preferred indirect method of grumbling and complaining to colleagues about whatever the problem is) must be eliminated.

Men are far more inclined to speak up, confront the issue or blow it off; it's not worth their time. It's not that men aren't tuned into behaviors of the past; they just don't allow issues to take over and engulf them.

Women are a bit different. They are less likely to speak up, confront it, not blow it off, and they allow whatever it is to fester or resurface in other areas. Women also assume (or possibly hope) that someone else will step forward and speak up and confront for them.

It's a type of domino factor. Instead of confronting the issue by communicating clearly to the person(s) who created the issue, women are more inclined to turn to other colleagues and friends and chat it up. Again and again. Wasted time.

If you don't speak up, you are liable to be blocked by others who do. A very vocal minority ends up ruling the roost.

It's all too common in today's workplace to not deal directly with the staboteur. Instead, management practices one of the great myths—leave it alone and it will go away. Of course, it only breeds.

If a manager, nurse, doctor, dentist ... whoever the health care professional is ... carries the traits of a Pit Bull, Skunk, Snake, Scorpion or Slug, deal with it. On the management side, address the culprit with desired behavior change and timeline to change, and if not successful, terminate.

As a co-worker, address the behavior, timeline to alter it and a consequence that you will do if there isn't a change. You can't fire them, but you sure don't have to play the enabling game either.

The Players ...

Pit Bulls are aggressive in their communication styles. That can be good news—they don't mumble (yes, they do shout at times); you can hear (and see) them coming; they are pushy, often blunt and can leave their recipients reeling and seething with whatever they are ranting about. Pit

Bulls come in all sizes and shapes, their bodies bulging with imaginary muscles and tattoos.

When you interact with a Pit Bull, being blunt is usually on your side. They actually don't like games and you can see (and often hear) them coming.

If a Pit Bull is in action and it's directed toward you, you wonder what in the hell you are doing taking this abuse ... if you wanted to be around grenades... you could have joined an army. Pit Bulls have no problem in letting you (and anyone else) know that they think you are a blithering idiot and moron.

Skunks are attractive to many. They look harmless and appear friendly. The last thing that you want to do in communicating with them is to show any type of hostility or aggression. That will set them into an automatic defensive response you may not like. They can be calmed and tamed by being deliberate and articulate in the communication style that they've signaled to you is the best receptor.

What you have to do is figure out which style it is. If you use the four key steps of communication—speaking clearly— loud enough so they can hear what is being said, connecting with them using phrases that are relevant, and asking for what you need, you'll most likely come out ahead.

Snakes are sometimes invisible, slithering along, supposedly doing their jobs until something catches their fancy and they rear their head and direct their attention to the target... you. You may not see them until they strike with both their tongue and fangs.

When they communicate, it can be subtle, like the rustling of some leaves that all of a sudden turn into a whirlwind and then "zap," you are it. They cruise along with their tails rattling a warning—don't mess with me. Or, their eyes can transform to mere slits, conveying to you and all that you're a blooming jerk and incompetent. Either way, they are in your face.

Scorpions have a very low tolerance for correction of their behaviors. Their attitude is that they know it all and they view themselves as unchangeable—they do things the way they do because "that's the nature of their beast." Scorpions like attention; they have an uncanny ability to fool management into thinking that they are vital to the workplace. When their bad behavior surfaces, it gets ignored or excused.

In communicating, they are the masters of passive aggression. They don't kick up much fuss in day to day interactions … but, out of the blue, when something riles them up, they strike. And when they strike, it's usually lethal.

In communicating with a Scorpion, be precise, have details and know what your consequences are if they continue to act/respond in their routine mode, because that's the way they've always done things … and gotten away with it.

Slugs are visible in every organization. They aren't Pit Bulls or bullies, don't like controversy and are minimalists in the communication department. The fact is that at times, Slugs look like "nobody" is home (or at work). Initially, they appear harmless. Their work life is riddled with maybes and I'll get to its... and then don't. Sometimes they are referred to as the "bless her hearts."

Slugs are deadly to the workplace. The good news is that your expectations are never let down; you don't expect them to do anything. The bad news is that their slacker behavior can become contagious. When communicating with them, make sure that they verbalize their understanding of what you said/requested, what steps they will do to respond to your request/statement and a time frame.

Summing Up

What is the bottom line when it comes to communication? First, moving beyond miscommunication, non-communication and wrong communication is critical.

Second, by not communicating a problem when it occurs, your silence says it's OK to continue doing whatever the activity is.

And third, neither men nor women are the "better" communicators. Both women and men must learn to be more flexible in their styles of speaking as well as in their interpretations and understandings of speaking. It is absurd to pretend otherwise or ignore the fact that there are communication differences between genders as well as cultures and generations.

> *JB's Keeper—*
>
> *Silence = Approval. Staboteurs know that if you don't speak up and speak out, your silence states your approval of the situation, whatever it may be.*

By encouraging others to speak up and out, you will significantly reduce miscommunication, nil/non-communication, and wrong communication in both your workplace and your personal life. The best news: staboteurs can't flourish in this environment. They count on "communication chaos" and a 'hands off" leadership team to breed.

9

The Art of the CarefrontingScript™ The New Way to Confront

I've learned to deal with it head-on ...
the price is too high not to. I will
never again compromise my
ethical and moral standards ... ever.
Survey Respondent #1057

How often do you wake up thinking, "Who can I go confront today?" "I rarely confront anyone" or "I never confront anyone" would be the most likely response.

One of the great myths surrounding conflict resolution is that if you leave it alone, it will go away. Get over that ... the only thing it does is fester. On the other hand ...

One of the great myths about *conflict* is that it must be solved immediately. Maybe, maybe not. It's not uncommon to put our mouths and actions in gear before the brain has really had the chance to kick-start.

Too many times, people jump in trying to resolve conflict without having the necessary data to do it. Data includes facts, assumptions, even what's circulating in the rumor mill. Who are all the players? They need to be involved in the process. Why does it need to be resolved? What are they cost factors to it? Is there a time frame within which it needs to be done?

Another of the great myths around conflict is that if there is any, there's something wrong with the workplace (or a relationship, for that matter). Do you possibly think that everyone is going to agree and/or get along 100 percent of the time? Conflict is normal. Get over this myth, too. The issue really is: Is it acknowledged? Is it dealt with?

There is also the belief that all conflicts must be resolved, no matter what; smile, shake hands, and let bygones be bygones. Nonsense.

Conflict and Anger ... Fallacies at Work

All these beliefs are misguided and usually wrong. Conflict arises in the workplace because people have different goals and objectives. Their perceptions vary. They hear differently. Culture, race and gender all play a part. There is also general "noise"—news, events, fear and concerns—that creates conflict. Most conflicts are believed to be rooted in some specific action or context. In reality, however, they are usually caused by communication failures or breakdowns.

Certainly there are variances. If you have a staboteur or saboteur in your midst, there is a deliberate provocation. And, when you can identify a situation in which another is purposely trying to hurt you, you need to confront him or her. And, you may need to get out ... either by working different days or a different shift—or working somewhere else.

Don't assume that you are going to be able to change this person; people only change because they choose to. Now, your reaction and actions could start them in the process, but you most likely will not have time to go through the series of processes that might enlighten her or him, nor may you want to.

JB's Keeper—

Conflict will not disappear completely from the workplace (or your personal life). It can be reduced by—

1. *Paying attention;* **recognize** *and* **identify** *difficulties, issues and concerns when they occur;*
2. *Determining if a problem* **needs** *intervention;*
3. *Acting—but only take action that is supported by information and knowledge of* **what should be done** *to get the best or ideal outcome;*
4. *Being prepared to react—which means you recognize that if the situation isn't going to change, you have a* **decision** *to make. Tolerate it or leave.*

Conflict Personas

I have identified several traits and characteristics of conflict. Whenever conflict escalates, it's normal for our concern to increase. And, when conflict is in play, the desire to win increases directly with the rise in self-interest. Saving face takes on an increased importance.

Handling it varies. Techniques that resolve it at a low level of conflict will most likely be ineffective and counterproductive at an intense or high level of conflict.

Here are the five key styles or modes of managing conflict:

- Competing
- Collaborating
- Accommodating
- Avoiding
- Compromising

You most likely have a persona or mode that is your preferred to handle conflict. You also have a back-up persona. It's not uncommon to handle something with the back-up first and, if that doesn't seem to be working, to transition into your "power" mode.

Each of the five styles has unique characteristics.

The *Competitive Style* is a good one to have in your corner when you are in a position of power. However, using a competitive style can alienate others. If you are someone of little power (or you are wrong or you have no support) in a disagreement with a co-worker or manager and you use a competitive style, you may find yourself without a job.

A competitive style doesn't work without power contacts and/or support behind you. When you feel that you have to make a decision and move quickly, using a competitive style does not necessarily mean that you are a bully or pushy.

Alternatively, using a *Collaborative Style* often encourages each person within the conflict to identify her needs and wants. A key factor to a successful collaboration involves identifying the needs and interests of the parties involved. When the issues are understood, it's easier to seek alternatives and compromises that will work for all.

The majority of health care professionals identify themselves as being collaborative. This style requires mutual respect and decent workplace relationships to succeed. And it requires time, lots of it. If any of these elements are missing, collaboration will fail.

The *Accommodating Style* usage indicates that the user likes to help or lend a hand, and often is someone who easily conforms. It's a style that works on a cooperative basis with another when asserting one's own claim for power. Accomodators like harmony in their workplaces.

When you invoke an accommodating style, it means that you are willing to set aside your own concern; you feel that you do not have a lot invested in the situation or the outcome. It is a perfect style to use when you feel that you are not losing too much by your giving up or backing off.

The *Avoiding Style* rears its head when you don't assert yourself, cooperate or ignore the conflict entirely. This also occurs when you feel that you are in a no-win situation, you don't want to be a bother, the whole problem or issue is irrelevant, you feel the other person has more power or is right, or, for whatever reason, you don't want to stick your neck out and take a position.

Some think that when others use avoidance to deal with conflict, they are being evasive or running away from the issue. Not necessarily so. Have you ever had a bad day when whatever comes out of your mouth is not glorious? There are times when an evasive or delaying tactic is appropriate and can be constructive. And some conflicts do resolve themselves when given breathing room.

The *Compromising Style* is in the center of the conflict management matrix. You end up giving up a little bit of what you want to get the rest of what you want. Compromising is usually the back-up to the Collaborative Style.

Everyone within the conflict does the same. To be successful in compromising, you need to clarify your needs and wants, as well as those of the other parties involved.

A compromising solution is reached when exchanges, concessions and bargaining are used to reach a conclusion that rarely satisfies everyone's concerns or objectives 100 percent. The solution, though, will meet the majority of each party's concerns and objectives.

One of the key differences between collaboration and compromise is that in collaboration you search for underlying needs and interests. In compromise, both sides end up giving up part of their needs and/or interests before a resolution is reached.

Where the goal in collaboration is usually a long-term win-win solution, in compromising, the outcome may more likely be short-term and expedient. At the end of a compromise, the normal response from the parties involved is, "I'm OK; I can live with the results."

Need additional help? Get *Zapping Conflict in the Health Care Workplace,* the companion to this book. Within it are extensive tools and descriptions for you to use in identifying your style, along with detailed descriptions of when and how to use them. It was revised in 2008.

The great majority of conflicts need to be confronted for a resolution. The sooner, the better. Very few resolve

Scenarios of the Conflict Managing Styles

Style	When it Works	When it Doesn't Work
Competitive	When you have the power and have to make a quick decision	When others don't respect your abilities or power; when there's plenty of time
Collaborative	When you have time; when you have a good relationship and respect	When there is a lack of trust and respect; when time is minimal
Accommodation	When the other person needs status; it's no big deal	When you need a real solution
Avoiding	When you must have the other person's participation; lots of time to readdress	When you have a lot to lose; when the other person is right; when you have nothing to contribute
Compromising	When both parties are right; when you want to keep the relationship going; when you are willing to give up some positioning	When only one party is right; when there is disparity in what "give ups" are in play

themselves or go away with no action. Think of conflicts and aging. They are life.

JB's Keeper—

***If someone betrays you once, it's her fault.
If someone betrays you twice, look in the mirror,
you've enabled it to happen ... it's your fault.
You must confront inappropriate
behavior and actions. Otherwise, it continues,
with your silent permission.***

Getting Ready to Confront

It's not uncommon to hold back, waiting for someone else to deal with the problem. Don't. Talking with another person face to face is usually the best way to confront a problem. That way, she can see your body language and you hers. You can observe whether she is listening. Some face-to-face confrontations require nerves of steel. You must be composed and have your facts together. Otherwise, emotions can erupt, and you end up either attacking or retreating. At that point the conflict only grows.

If meeting face to face is impossible, writing becomes your second best choice. But, writing has drawbacks. You can't be sure that she will read your letter (or e-mail). Tones are missed (and misinterpreted in e-mails and letters). Writing does, though, give you an opportunity to set out the facts as you understand them and to let the other party know how you have been affected by her action.

Before you send any letters, have a confidante read over your words to eliminate undue sharpness or overemotional responses. This is a time to explain, rationally, how you perceive the facts. If you wait too long to confront, you're at a disadvantage. The other party may be clueless as to what she did, or why you are upset about it.

Avoid confronting others on the phone. If you do so, you can't be sure that she is really listening to what you say. In fact, she could put you on hold, walk away, or even hang up before you are aware the line has been disconnected and you could just go on talking. Even if you both remain on the line, you are unable to see her face, her eyes and her body expressions. Nor can she see yours. She is unable to visibly see your anger or your hurt. She may hear it through your tone, but that's no guarantee.

JB's Keeper—

*When you observe conflict-creating behavior,
whether directed at you or somewhere else,
be conscious of it. Be aware that it contributes
to destructive role modeling. Ask yourself,*

1. **Is this really a conflict … or is it just some confusion?**
2. **Should I be putting time and energy into it?**
3. **Why should I?**

*If you determine that it is true conflict and
a problem, take overt action—immediately.
But, if you question whether you should be
involved, you probably shouldn't be.
And, you really have to decide how much
time and energy you are willing to put into it.*

Clues and Cues to What's Been Said

Communicating how you feel, what you feel and why you feel the way you do can be challenging. You may think you are incredibly clear and precise—yet the listener could easily be putting a "spin" on it internally. Communicating about conflict requires you to pay attention to verbal and nonverbal clues and cues—some come across loud and clear, others are disguised in body language, posturing, tone and words.

- *Tap into your intuition ... what are your gut feelings saying and what do you perceive is going on?* Your intuition is at work, trust it. If you feel internally that there is distrust, negativity or distancing, there most likely is.
- *Are there any discrepancies in what the other person is saying? Is there a sharpness or other inflection to the kind of tone used? Is body language open or closed or giving other hints that might counter what's being verbally said?* If she is all smiles, yet arms are crossed, her body is turned away, and she speaks sharply, the smile doesn't match the rest of her. Don't trust her.
- *Is there someone you trust that you can bounce the situation off of and get feedback?* When you are close to something or it's very important to you, you may overreact or misinterpret what you see or hear. Other eyes and ears are helpful.

Your CarefrontingScript™

Back in the eighties, after the publication of my first book on bad behavior in the workplace and conflict resolution in the workplace (*Woman to Woman: From Sabotage to Support*), I started to use the words "carefront" and "carefronting" in my programs. I thought it was a unique twist on the word "confront" and my experience and research showed that women were more confrontationally adverse than men were. I wanted to soften the concept a bit as I presented it to my largely female audiences. Carefronting vs. confronting. They liked it. So did I.

Little did I know that David Augsburger, author of *Caring Enough to Confront* and professor of Pastoral Care and Counseling at Fuller Theological Seminary in California, had created and used "carefront" back in the seventies. I was disappointed to learn that the two of us shared a small publisher yet had actually never met. More disappointed that I didn't know that he had created this terrific word until years later.

Augsburger's model focuses more on family relationships, faith and forgiveness. He wasn't writing about the workplace, but what he says certainly relates to it.

Associate Professor Betty Kupperschmidt teaches theory and clinical courses at the University of Oklahoma College of Nursing. She, too, has included the basis of Augsburger's model in numerous presentations and several publications. According to Kupperschmidt,

> We have an ethical mandate to care enough to confront. The ANA Code of Ethics clearly reads that each individual RN (not just the managers) is responsible to 1) participate in attaining and maintaining a professional practice environment (Provision 6) and 2) address her own conflicts in a way that preserves their personal integrity.

When I do training sessions and workshops on conflict, I bring laminated cards for participants that include the CarefrontingScript™ dialogue. Many hole punch them and add them to the back of their badges—when they come across a situation that needs addressing, out come the cards.

This script is so much better than the standard conflict resolution dialogue supported by HR and training professionals in HR. The standard dialogue is limp and has no zip to it. It goes ...

When you ...

I felt ...

Because ...

In the future ...

Boring, it's dated and very ineffective. Why? It doesn't "call out" the creator of the action; it doesn't get a buy-in from the other party to change; it doesn't offer any consequence if there isn't a change.

Imagine trying to change a child's behavior. The standard dialogue would go something like this ...

Luke, *when you* were late coming home from school,
I felt worried *because* I thought you had been hurt.
In the future, always call me before you go to your friend's house.

OK, Luke might hear that you are worried and he might hear you say to check in before doing anything. But, how can you be sure? Change the script.

The CarefrontingScript™ dialogue that I'm giving you has taken more than 20 years to perfect. It adds three simple lines to the old dialogue. The result is to the point, gets a buy-in and, as every parent knows when he or she tries to change an unwanted activity or behavior, it gives a consequence if it's not done. Does it work? You bet. One hospital in Texas implemented it and saw a remarkable hike in employee satisfaction evals within a three month period.

Your new lines will be for the CarefrontingScript ...

Was it your intent ... ?

Are you (or will you be) committed ... ?

If there isn't a change, I'll ...

Let's go back to eight year-old Luke. When inserting the three new lines, here's how the new scripting goes ...

Luke, *when* you were late coming home from school, I *felt* worried *because* I thought you had been hurt.

Was it your intent to make Mommy worry? (Do not say anything until Luke responds in some way.)

In the future, always call me before you go to your friend's house to get permission.

Are you committed to call me? (Again, do not say anything until Luke responds yes, no, maybe, or shrugs.)

If there isn't a change, there's no skateboarding for a month.

Now, which version do you think is going to get Luke's buy-in? The first, where there is no calling for any commitment and no consequence, or the latter?

Luke's a kid. Would this work with a co-worker or a staff member? Yes.

Let's say that you've got a co-worker who's a Slug. Bertha's nicey nice when all is going her way, but gets easily riled if things don't or if she has to do anything extra.

She is routinely late for work and takes double the time for a break than would normally be allocated. For Bertha, moving and responding to the everyday demands of the workplace normally is in "slow motion" when compared to co-workers. She's a classic Slug.

You are tired of being her cover and feeling that you are walking on eggshells when dealing with her. Your script could go something like this ...

> Bertha, *when you* were late last Monday, Wednesday and Thursday by an hour, *I was* ticked *because I feel* that you weren't concerned about adequate patient coverage nor do you care that you were adding stress to the rest of us because we have to cover for you.

> *Was it your intent to put stress on the rest of the team and not be there for our patients?* (Do not say anything until Bertha responds in some way—most likely, she will deny and/or say that there's a misunderstanding of some sort.)

> *In the future,* I expect you to be here when your shift starts. *Are you committed to being here on time?* (Again, do not say anything until she reponds yes, no, or maybe.) *If you aren't and there isn't a change,* I won't cover for you any longer.

Confronting isn't a piece of cake. But, it must be done. Otherwise, you create a movie dialogue in your head, spend hours (sometimes days/weeks/months) on whatever the issue/problem is, most likely grumble about it with co-workers who all will agree the person is a real jerk ... and then nothing is done to get resolution. With the CarefrontingScript™, you are an adult.

CarefrontingScript™

When you _____ .
    (What was the action?)

I felt _____ .
    (What was your reaction—were you angry, upset, feeling betrayed?)

Because _____ .
    (What does it look, sound or feel like—does it look like the person never credits anyone on the team, does it sound like she purposely spreads rumors, or does it feel like she is deliberately stabotaging the team?)

Was it your intent to _____ ?
    (Repeat what the action was ... then STOP!!! Do not respond until there is a response from the other side.)

In the future _____ .
    (What behavior do you want to see? Be specific—say what you want.)

Are you committed to _____ ?
    (What you want them to do.)

If there isn't a change, _____ .
    (What's the consequence—for example, will you include everyone on the email distribution list so credit is appropriately given?)

This won't roll off your tongue without practice and use. But, as you begin to use it, you will be amazed at how effective it is. The perfect addition to your bag of workplace tools.

JB's Keeper—

When a workplace becomes the pits, get out. Don't rearrange the deck chairs on the Titanic. Women are more inclined to hang on, feeling that the job/work/boss, etc., needs them. Don't. Health care for the next 20 plus years offers plenty of opportunities to move about. Staying put because you "need the money" doesn't fly either. Jobs that pay good money are being offered elsewhere. Open your eyes, your ears, and start networking.

If you are in a situation where you strongly believe that another person is purposely trying to harm you physically, psychologically or professionally, get out. If you want to practice confronting, give it a shot. But be forewarned. It's improbable that you will have the time to go through a series of processes that might enlighten the other party. Or want to.

Move on. You are better off gathering up your marbles and finding another field to play in. Don't expect to change her ways. Working in a toxic environment will eventually make you sick. Start looking now; there is another job out there. When you move on, the only regret you'll have is that you didn't leave sooner.

Don't Be a Performer

The final step in changing stabotaging behavior is to act on your commitment to not be a player in the game. Don't just talk about it. That's too easy. Put a bite behind your bark. When someone does something that is not acceptable, say so. Carefront it. If you see another doing it, call her on her action. To her face.

Sure, it's scary. But consider the consequences. In the survey, sabotaged women have reported everything from their reputations being destroyed, termination, being accused of stealing narcotics to (even in one case) accused of murder. Must the workplace be so toxic? No. The choice is yours.

The Players ...

Pit Bulls are the scariest when it comes to confrontations. Because they snarl, bark and bite, you know that there will most likely be some kind of counter back. When you use the CarefrontingScript™ though, you are able to be articulate, cite specifically what the issue is and put them on the spot. "Was it your intent ... (to be the jerk, to take credit, to discredit a co-worker, etc.)"

You see, the "Was it your intent ..." line is so powerful that it stops even a Pit Bull in her tracks. She (or he) shuts the mouth; she has to chew a bit on your words. No one talks to her that way. You continue with your script, getting her commitment to alter the action and then let her know what you will do if she doesn't.

Don't waste your time confronting anyone unless you intend to follow through with the consequence side. I know, I know. This is really the hardest part. But it will change how she deals with you in the future.

Skunks may actually seem like they welcome your input and want to make the workplace a better place. That is until they realize that you are serious about whatever you are saying ... and they are the target of it. Then it can get stinky.

With a Skunk, it's critical to let them know how their action looks/feels/sounds. Because they are "fluffy" at times, how others might perceive them matters. Then continue with your script with the intent, commitment and consequence.

Snakes are totally reactionary. Your confrontation may be very threatening. Before they coil up and strike, practice what you want to say. It's important to get the "When you," "I felt," "Because" and "Was it your intent" out quickly. The "intent" portion will slow/stop them, just as it does the Pit Bull. "What do you mean did I intend...?"

The first person who speaks out after the "Was it your intent" line is delivered will usually lose the confrontation. In negotiating, it's called "The Blink Factor." Don't let it be you. Snakes will uncoil and slither away, hissing every once in awhile, but you got your point across.

Scorpions share a lot of similarities to Snakes. Both are covert, independent and not into team playing. Working in health care demands team work. No exceptions. Scorpions have to be confronted immediately when their behaviors are inappropriate. Otherwise, any action, or reaction, is a result of their ongoing nature.

Slugs are the "Bless Her Hearts" of the workplace. They are just there and tolerated by most. Slugs don't get confronted much; co-workers and managers step around them or just avoid them—it's too much work, and why bother? They just shift and mold back to what their sluggish selves were.

Slugs should be confronted when their behaviors and performances merit. Why should they get a free pass? You may think, "Well, because they don't strike back, stink up the place, sting or bite like the others." Yet their mediocre performances are just as cancerous. Slugs bring down the productivity of the workplace. It's a slow death.

The CarefrontingScript™ works well with them. Make sure that you have details to support the "When you..."; that they respond to the "Was it your intent..."; that they buy-in to "Are you committed..." (if they don't and you are a manager, push to terminate as soon as possible); and when you say, "If there isn't a change..." make sure your consequence has some meaning to them so it gets their attention.

Summing Up

Conflicts and confrontations are a series of moves and countermoves with all who are involved. Think of a dance: some are short; some have a variety of movements; some are out of synch; and some flash and dazzle.

Confronting someone takes responsibility and courage. It involves accountability: for all parties involved. For you, it means you have to deal with it and take action; for the other person(s), being responsive and accountable for whatever the events were. If you do not confront the person who creates offending behavior or actions, your silence condones it.

The American Nurses Association's Code of Ethics for Nurses states,

"Each professional nurse has an ethical duty to resolve workplace conflicts."

Precise and to the point.

As you learn more about yourself and the people you work with, you will be able to act with more power, courage and confidence. Mastering conflict and confrontation will be part of your formula. Doing it and using the CarefrontingScript™ will create a positive workplace.

10

It Takes a Village to Create a Team ... the **Great,** the **Good** and the **Ugly**

Team is more than just
a four-letter word; it is a
different way of making decisions,
of doing the work, and of relating
to each other. In today's turbulent and
complex health care workplace, the
successful leaders and employees will be
those who understand team and work
together in partnership with their colleagues.
Dr. Jo Manion
Create a Positive Health Care Workplace

The big three in every organization are better communications, reducing conflict and effective team work. Teams come in all sizes and shapes ... some work within the same department within the same building; some are remote and miles apart, connected by technology.

When a workplace isn't clicking, morale plummets, loyalties go out the door, distrust grows, stress increases, productivity nosedives, management is viewed as inept, and good and great staff and managers leave.

An article published in the *Harvard Business Review* revealed that when employees ranked their satisfaction scale within the workplace with a range from being "very/extremely" satisfied (a 5) to being "good" satisfied (a 4), the ones that marked just "good" were *six times* as likely to defect to a competitor than those who were "very/extremely" satisfied with their workplaces and jobs.

If there are dissatisfied employees, management has got to get off its tush and figure out why. In some cases, it's the employees who are the grumblers and basically little will satisfy them, not even tripling wages. Get rid of them. In most cases, that's not the reason. Let's start with the possibility of inept management.

In a previous study for *Zapping Conflict in the Health Care Workplace*, 47 percent of employees who had quit reported doing so because of poor management. The present study, done five years later, shows a significant increase to 63 percent quitting because of poor management!

Staff expects management to deal with problems. Issues that could be tied to the workplace environment, inequities, toxic co-workers, etc. If management turns its back, then staff views that management as an enabler and incompetent. Where it should be part of the solution, it becomes part of the problem.

When's a Team Not a Team?

The phrase *team player* almost has a tainted air about it for many. In the past, it meant keeping your mouth shut,

---

JB's Keeper—

Very Satisfied *employees are your internal and external cheerleaders.*

Satisfied *employees really have little or no stories of bravo about their workplace or management ... a job is a job.*

Dissatisfied *employees are your nightmare ... their stories will take you down.*

---

working long hours, and not speaking up when someone else took the credit.

It's essential to understand that each member of the team has the potential to be a *Key Player*, no matter the size and number of work locations of the team.

A *Key Player* carries out her job at a peak performance plus. She can be found at any level of an organization. She does any job with unswerving excellence, and her team skills make her an essential member of her team. She is innovative and gives more than 100 percent to the effort, problems are seen and solutions are offered, and being responsible and accountable are as normal as breathing.

Key Players are confident, don't participate in the creation or spreading of rumors or gossip, share unwritten rules of the workplace, acknowledge the work of others on the team, and are not conflict creators or staboteurs.

Key Players have a unique combination of skills, are essential and can't be easily replaced. If one walked into the room, all would know who and what she was. In the end, she has more leverage, is presented with extra choices and opportunities, and has greater autonomy in shaping her own career than her co-workers who merely show up and punch the clock.

Good Players, not Key Players, make up the majority of most workplaces. Remember, these are the ones that are most likely to leave if a better appetizing carrot is dangled in front of them. They see problems, but are unclear on solutions and they need ongoing support. What Good Players share with Key Players is that they are responsible and accountable. Although they don't have the loyalty quotient that the Key Player does, they are still usually efficient, effective and productive.

Unfortunately, workplaces aren't perfect and they have the mediocre or *Ugly Player*—too many of them on both the staff and management sides. From one end of the spectrum to the other, Ugly Players see others as the problem, never offer viable solutions and are non-accountable and non-responsible.

Mediocrity breeds more mediocrity. Your good players can turn into the mediocre through a workplace's benign neglect. The Ugly move in. Poor performance becomes accepted: "Oh, that's just Bertha (or Bert)," or "You know how Bertha is," or "Bless her heart, she does try ..." The Ugly employee is a downer for the workplace. Her behavior affects morale, loyalty, trust, productivity and turnover.

Management is viewed as totally inept because it tolerates/allows it. Every once in awhile, management steps up to the plate and confronts the behavior. The creator promises to change, then the yo-yo factor kicks in. Good this week, pissy the next. Then a begging for another chance. Good the next week, pissy the following. You get the picture.

When an Ugly Player is in motion, management often enables her actions. Reasons include:

- If I ignore it, it will go away.
- It's been going on for so long, we can tolerate it.
- If I do something, I might get sued.
- If I do something, it will effect the bottom line.
- I'll deal with it when the behavior gets really bad.

Deleting Mediocrity from Your Workplace

Workplaces need to address the poor performers—the Slugs of the workplace. It's done by creating a culture that clearly states, "This is a no-tolerance zone. We don't tolerate rotten behavior; we don't tolerate mediocrity." A written code of conduct is needed that emphasizes the type of conduct, attitude and respect you want in the workplace. Consequences should be included for violating the code.

Years ago, the American Hospital Association published *In Your Hands*. In it, the phrase, "employer of choice" was birthed. Sounds great, but it's not complete. Today's workplace should strive to be the "employer of choice of choice employees." Mediocrity, the Ugly Players, the Slugs are not welcome.

Tie all aspects of performance, including interpersonal communication with co-workers and conduct, to financial rewards. Who says everyone gets an automatic pay increase? Document problems and expectations in performance reviews and make sure the employee gets a copy.

Before the towel is thrown in, it's common for management and co-workers to try and "fix it," whatever fix it Bertha needs. Ask,

- Is Bertha worth saving? Does she contribute more than she takes away?

- Can she change or is she beyond help?
- Why should you help her?

No team is without problems. What happens when you are involved with a team and it just doesn't get off the dime, or when certain members don't carry their share of the load and others seem to dominate? On any team, whether newly formed or established, there will be breakdowns in communication, tasks and cohesion.

Take Roxanne. She works on the administrative side of a very large health care system located in the East. One of the system's projects was one of mentoring with a local community college with financial assistance for tuition. A committee comprised of several members, both staff and directors, acted as the oversight and supervising of the nursing students in the program. Roxanne felt it was very worthwhile and she expected to be on the committee. She shares ...

One of our members resigned from the committee because of her workload, then she came back. The person who left wasn't the same one who returned. She was now confrontational, abusive, a bully and potstirrer.

The program was one of the "gems" of our organization, yet was feeling like jagged glass to those who kept it going. Meetings, which always take time, became the place not to be. She would nitpick anything and everything we did and said. She became a master at sending abusive emails to me personally, and would copy everyone on the team.

One year I was chair. A thank-you letter had been addressed to me for all the work that had been done. I made copies for everyone on the team. She insisted that I go back and ask for individual letters addressed to each committee member thanking them.

This was ongoing over a nine-month period. I finally went to HR with copies of e-mails and details of ongoing activities that blocked the team and began to affect my own workload. The response was negligible. HR and the staff members of the executives, who spent hours weekly on this committee, paid no attention; they were passive and avoiders.

For me, it was mentally and physically exhausting. I finally withdrew from my committee and actually sought work with another VP, who recognized what an abusive environment it had become.

As I look back, all I see is dysfunction, dysfunction and more dysfunction. I finally realized that the person I was dealing with was in need of help and that I wasn't the "cause" of her responses that resulted in putting others down in order to advance her own personal agenda. She was power-hungry.

Whether you are a member of a team or it's leader, it's important to recognize problems when they are just beginning. Roxanne had dual roles of being on a committee and later its chair.

Common problems include fragmentation, lack of productivity, lack of motivation, resentment, misbehavior, dominating and submissive personalities, overdependence on the leader, too much accommodation and too little challenging, lack of interest, and failure to deal with conflict. These are all problems that will surface at various times throughout the evolution of any team.

As a leader or as a member, you must not ignore any problem. Avoidance should be squashed. The adage "anything worthwhile is worth working for" applies.

Teams at Work

For any team to succeed, all the players must have a common vision and the desire to succeed at their goal. Players must complement each other, recognizing that not everyone has the same strengths and weaknesses, and being prepared to compensate for or offset others' weaknesses.

Brian Lee is the author of *Keep Your Nurses & Health Care Professionals for Life!* and CEO of Custom Learning Systems based in Calgary, Alberta, Canada. He's the creator of the Service Excellence drive that many hospitals participate in.

Brian is an enthusiast for creating empowered workplaces and enabling employees to also do their best. He believes that there is a strong link between employee morale and customer satisfaction and often quotes Press Ganey, "A one percent change in employee morale equals a two percent change in patient satisfaction." Brian states,

> Give the staff the gift of empowerment ... treat them as adults. A revolution is occurring that puts the value of a staff's attitude ahead of clinical competence when it comes to how managers treat staff and how staff treats patients (and/or customers).

Jo Manion completed her doctoral work on the joy of working. She's authored several books including *Create a Positive Health Care Workplace!* and *From Management to Leadership*. During her career, she's been a staff nurse, faculty member, director of nursing and administrator. Today, she is a nationally recognized speaker and consults exclusively to health care organizations. She shares an experience in which she was brought in as part of a recognition day for staff ...

The executive team was told by an outside consultant that it was important for them to recognize staff. The nursing managers were asked to identify those that were exemplary, then set up a big event to recognize them. The chief nurse would identify the honorees at the event. Just before the chief nurse was introduced, the CEO asked her to cut her remarks short.

All the honorees heard the request and instead of recognition, ended up getting a coupon for a free meal in the cafeteria. The Board adjourned to a private room for a catered lunch. It would have been better to have totally ignored them instead of treating them like cattle.

When People Bug You

All of us, at some time in our careers, have worked with people who drove us nuts. Why? You name it—there's a long laundry list out there.

If you work with someone who bugs you, ask yourself why ... what is it that he or she does that pushes your button? Make a list. Is it an annoying habit or mannerism? Most can be ignored. Quality of work cannot.

Identify and list her strengths. Why do you think she was hired? What are her skills? Separate the personal issues from the professional ones.

Ask yourself, "What's in it for me to work with her? What's in it for her to work with me?" Don't think about whether you want to be friends. Friendship is a bonus, not a requirement of the workplace. Consider her talents instead.

If her work involves or overlaps your work, wouldn't you like to see her accomplish what she needs to do, before it all comes crashing into your arena? And, if her mannerisms, habits or traits have no impact on whether she gets her job done or bugs others, then let go—this is not something you need to direct your energy toward. Choose a battle that's worth fighting for.

The Grumpies at Work

A bad attitude is different from a bad hair day. It doesn't change with something as simple as a shampoo and cut. Something has to be done. If you are the team leader, part of your responsibility is to keep the group's productivity at a certain level. If someone's actions are dragging it down, it's up to you to stop the behavior before other team members start turning on each other, as well as on her—and, believe it or not, on you.

Whether she's a co-worker or someone you manage, get out your note pad. Document. Start to write down examples, and cite lots of them. You will need to confront her privately. Don't expect a one-time mention to change her; expect to repeat your examples at a later confrontation. If she denies her behavior, don't be surprised. She has been doing it for a long time. It's part of her. The bottom line is that action is needed. When someone has a bad attitude, it's like cancer. It can destroy a team if untreated.

JB's Keeper—

Ugly and grumpy people don't make your day or your workplace. They are the energy suckers—always chipping away at something or someone. Do yourself a favor and minimize your contact.

When a conflict creator or staboteur's motivation is confronted and redirected, the team has the ability to be rebirthed and revamped. She won't like to be left out in the cold for long and may actually attempt to make amends and rejoin your team. If she doesn't, you know she doesn't belong there.

Finally, the old saying "If you give her enough rope, she will hang herself" may apply. Once you identify your troublemaker, you must sidestep her games. Being a staboteur and conflict creator takes a lot of time, energy and commitment. It takes away from her work and the work she is committed to do. The longer the game goes on, the less is produced, and the more likely the culprit will be exposed to co-workers and managment. Who, in turn, will reduce the enabling of the behaviors by confronting the creator.

A Star Team Was Born

In *Zapping Conflict in the Health Care Workplace*, I featured the remarkable turnabout of the nursing staff of Kaiser Permanente in Hayward, California under the visionary leadership of Debora Zachau, the former director of Patient Care Services. With a turnover in the high teens, the staff was able to reduce it to low single digits within a fairly short period of time.

In summary, what Debora and her team did was:

- Created off-site programs with national speakers— I spent a week there delivering the *Zapping Conflict* program for all staff.
- Used *The Four Agreements* by Don Miguel Ruiz as a values foundation for all managers.
- Identified and purchased books for all staff that tied into the new program including *The Four Agreements* and *FISH*.

- Implemented ongoing internal celebrations and events that all managers participated in and were delivered to staff during all shifts (latte and tea breaks delivered via a cart, ice cream sundaes, 15-minute chair massages).

Traditionally, employees in different departments can be likened to a foreign country—nobody talks to anyone outside of their area. That all changed. Because they all get together every month, they face each other, communication skills are improving and distrust has been reduced.

The program cost money—almost $1,000,000 was budgeted over a three-year period (the books alone were over $50,000). Because of the huge reduction in turnover related costs, the organization was able to recoup the amount several times over within the first year. They knew that in order to save money and reduce the millions spent in annual replacement costs, they had to spend money.

Teams Need Courageous Leaders

Courage and leadership are soul mates. The director of Surgical Services for Emmanuel Hospital in Oregon is a perfect example of how the two work together.

When I first had the opportunity to work with Cheryl Purvis, it was in her capacity of director of Women's Services for five of the hospitals under the Legacy Health System umbrella. It was very clear to me that she was a no-nonsense person when she said to her managers before our workshop began ...

If you have a performance or behavior problem with an employee, we need to address it fearlessly. We can start out by coaching for success, but if they have not an interest or ability to change, we need to document

it and I will support you. I will not leave you hanging
out there.

Within a few weeks of the training program I gave for
her and her team, seven had resigned from one unit. This
can be scary, until you look at the flip side. If those women
weren't willing to go forward with her vision and what
was agreed upon by the majority that this was what they
wanted to look and act like, would you want them on your
team? No. What Cheryl said was ...

> At first it was scary; then we realized we had
> a tremendous opportunity to hire and reshape
> the team and management where we wanted and
> needed it to go. It was a gift.

During that time, a new hospital was birthing, Legacy
Salmon Creek in Washington. Hiring was unique; attitude
and behavior were part of the core foundation of all hires.
Yes, clinical skills were important. But if the candidate
didn't have the collaborative attitude, an attitude that practiced what was best for the team, the candidate was the
wrong fit. No hire. They had far more candidates than
positions available. Cheryl continues ...

> The manager, Gretchen Amacher, and I did
> behavioral interviewing. We asked about experience—
> tell us about the best team you've ever been on, and
> what made it the best; describe a time when it was
> difficult to give feedback to a co-worker or manager;
> tell me about the co-worker, manager or doctor who
> was difficult to work with or communicate with;
> describe a situation you found frustrating; and, how
> did you handle it?

They would be asked to describe how they responded to conflict. If they answered that they tried to avoid it, we knew that they weren't into conflict resolution. We asked, 'What pushed their buttons?' and how they responded when it happened. Tone in their responses was important.

People who didn't already work within the Legacy Health System didn't always question why they were turned down. If they were current employees within the Legacy System and asked, 'Why?' they were told why. Some were offended. Several of those actually kicked into gear and made changes within their current Legacy workplaces. One nurse said to her co-workers after she was turned down, 'Do you know what our reputation is? What others are saying about us? How our team could really be functioning?'

Those are just a few of the questions used in a telling face to face interview. They make statements, followed by a question. Cheryl gives an example ...

...You just came on duty; you get the report and heard about a difficult patient and family. You now find out that the patient is yours. You are walking into the patient's room for the first time that shift, what are you going to say?

According to Cheryl Purvis, the people she would hire would say something like, "It's a new day, I'm your nurse. I understand you had a rough night. Is there anything I can do for you this morning?"

Health care professionals are highly judgemental. The profession demands that decisions be made quickly—at times—judgements are made. She says that judgement needs to relapse; we need to listen to what the patient is *really* saying.

With this first printing, Salmon Creek is two years out. The Organization Development team continues to interact with employees to make sure that all stay on track. Pre-opening, they asked each employee and manager what they wanted their departments and units to look like, be like.

Two years later, post evals show that, amazingly, the staff strongly feels that they have actually achieved what their ideal was. There is huge employee and patient satisfaction—in the top 10 percent, according to national benchmarking. There are 85 RN's who staff the unit; an incredible two-thirds of them were personally recruited by the staff. Why? Simply this: they wanted to retain the same sense of team-work and commitment to quality that they did. As Cheryl Purvis, director extraordinaire says, "Completely amazing. No hiring problems in that unit!"

Behavior hiring can make or break the team, the hos-pital. It takes guts, courage, and a team with vision.

The Players ...

Pit Bulls are vocal and visible on every team. If anyone is going to put a label on another, bullies and Pit Bulls are commonly linked. Savvy co-workers learn to stay out of their way when on a rampage. They are intimidating, used to having their way and will openly firehose new ideas that are introduced to the team, the organization.

Pit Bulls don't like surprises. Co-workers learn that if they get the Pit Bull involved early on in any change process, they are more likely to buy-in vs. citing the way things used to be. Otherwise, the Pit Bull is a team of one. When conflict is brewing, they usually don't see themselves as the cause or instigator. If they do, then their attitude is that their way is the only way, the right way; therefore, there shouldn't be a problem. Pit Bulls put little value in teambuilding activities, since being a team player isn't crucial for them.

Skunks are very visible within any team. They don't shirk from the limelight and will step forward and take credit if a fellow team member hesitates. They like to help out, as long as it benefits them. Skunks will openly participate in teambuilding activities, they enjoy the social side of the workplace and are happy campers when all seems to be going their way. When it doesn't, or they perceive that things aren't going their way, their covert side surfaces. They can put up quite a stink.

Snakes slide along on the outside of a team, rarely moving into the center until they feel that they are threatened or being attacked. Once there, they are impossible to miss and there's little one can do to stop their fast moving strike. A strike by a Snake can be fatal; its prey is often a new employee. Once in a while, it will rear its head to test the air, then pull back. Snakes don't volunteer for anything, preferring to stay out of management's eye.

Scorpions share similarities with the Snake ... they are both covert and their attack can be lethal. Where the Snake rises and is impossible to miss as it strikes, the Scorpion stings its victim, with few knowing what happened. Or exactly when. Scorpions are difficult team members. Preferring to work in the shadows, they are more about "Leave me alone, I do my job. If you get in my way, it's your problem, not mine."

Slugs are the "What me worry?" of the workplace and team. Never proactive, they will wait to see how others respond and then react to circumstances. Slugs don't take the lead on anything—it's too risky and besides, if they did, they might stand out. More could be expected of them, which is not what they want. They are inclined to go along with the majority. but will grumble and complain along the way. Slugs come in all shapes, sizes and ages.

Summing Up

Teams are not created overnight. Most take months or even years to pull together.

Creating the ideal village—a necessity for any high performing team to be productive in the workplace—demands that the environment is respectful, has clear communication and conflict-handling skills, has trust within staff and administration levels, and is non-game playing. Negativity is downplayed and staff are empowered to make decisions.

When workplaces create a no-tolerance of bad behavior policy and eliminate the Pit Bulls, Skunks, Snakes, Scorpions and Slugs, loyalty and morale within increases, trust builds and stress is reduced, productivity increases and teams are strengthened. The final result is that turnover drops and management is viewed as caring and proactive. The workplace becomes one of choice and attracts the Keepers; no critters allowed.

11

My Final Thoughts ...

Dealing with conflict and
Staboteurs is about choice ... yours.
Dr. Judith Briles

Stabotage and sabotage costs any organization money. Sometimes in the millions of dollars. Collectively, within the health care industry, billions.

For individuals, it creates a rotten work environment that leads to higher levels of stress, lower productivity and morale.

Bad behavior can be calculated financially. It also can be resolved and eliminated. Both management and staff must take their heads out of the sand—and acknowledge that bad behavior exists, gather and learn the tools to confront it, and confront and deal with it.

Whether you are an organization or an individual, you do this by ...

1. Waking up and acknowledging that behavior problems exist;
2. Identifying individuals and/or departments that are the creators;
3. Documenting their actions clearly;
4. Meeting with them and state the behaviors/issues, what your expectations are, the time frame that improvements and changes must be completed by, and the consequences if they aren't;
5. Using my CarefrontingScript™ model; and
6. Remembering this is about your business (or yourself), this isn't the time to invoke a buddy-buddy style: this is serious. So, keep pleasantries to a minimum.

Why an organization chooses to kiss off millions of dollars a year and keep its head in the sand is beyond me. Ditto for why anyone would choose to stay in a workplace that is toxic and debilitating. Today's successful hospitals now know rotten attitudes and behaviors can have a far more negative effect on their facilities and patients than one with inferior clinical skills.

It's scary holding staff and co-workers accountable. It involves risk. Former President John F. Kennedy said, "There is risk and costs to a program of action ... There are far more risks to a program of inaction."

When action is taken, here's what happens: morale, loyalty and productivity increase, teams are strengthened, stress is reduced, distrust disappears; turnover nosedives, management is viewed as proactive and buckets of money are saved.

It's your choice. Choose.

If you would like to create a workplace of choice employees, it would be my honor to work with your group.

Judith Briles

Acknowledgments

While it is an author with a vision who conceives a book, that book cannot be delivered without the help of a birthing team. *Stabotage!* carries key elements from *Zapping Conflict in the Health Care Workplace,* coupled with an extensive, new survey and new steps and material for unraveling sabotage and conflict in the health care workplace.

The thousands of women and men who work in the health care field have been generous with their time and insights beyond anything I could imagine. I thank the survey respondents and those who agreed to be interviewed. Their voices make this book. When appropriate, names have been changed to respect requests and the need for confidentiality.

And huge thanks to my health care encouragers, cronies, conference pals and meeting planning visionaries—Jo Manion,

Diann and Tom Uustal, Leslie Brock, Ellen Tryon, Kathy Uran, Wendy Alexander, Sharon Cox, Karyn Cousart, ML Hanson, Michael Zabinski, and Peggy and Richard Ireland.

A few years ago, I had just completed speaking at a conference and fell on a glob of ice cream that someone had dropped and left on a marble floor. With the help of chemicals, I was able to show up and complete speaking and consulting contracts, each time wondering what did I do and what did I say. One long-term client who knew me well said when I arrived at his facility, "You look like shit." He was right. Many times, I felt and said, "I don't think I can do this anymore." In late 2006, I thought it was over and that I wouldn't be able to mentally or physically work again.

For two years, I wasn't able to write or read in any depth or tweak things the way I used to. Over this two year period of time, I was in the hospital ten times and had three surgeries. Few but my closest friends understand the depth of my challenges. Today, my eyes aren't perfect, but are now so much better. My head isn't perfect, but is now so much better. My lower back isn't perfect, but is now so much better. My speaking was affected for some time, but now, it's as good as ever. I know what my limitations are, but I'm back.

I'm greatful that I'm beginning to function again and couldn't have done it without the team of many, many doctors and health care professionals. So an extra round kudos to the good doctors Stanley Gingsburg, Gary Morris, Jennifer Crismon, Joel Goldstein, Lynn Hellerstein, Terri Heble, Theodore Curtis, Douglas Dennis, Barbara Briggs and the many eye and physical therapists who got me walking, moving and seeing once again.

Books can't be done without the artists. Huge thank-yous to Rebecca Finkel who saw my vision so quickly for the

Stabotage! cover; Shannon Parish for bringing the stabotage culprits to life in her creative illustrations for my workshops; Ronnie Moore who always knows how to visually present any book for the reader; master editors Barb Munson and John Maling for the right tweaking and challenges; Cameron Fay and the entire Friesens' team for being the best in the printing business; and my publishing pals Rick Frishman, John Kremer, David Hancock and Brian Jud.

And of course, none of my books are created without the support of my staff John Maling and Dolores Ruybal. As always, all my books are started and finished around water. In the past, my body of water of choice was at the beach. The accident I had limited my travel. So this water body requirement started with hot tub submersions several times a day—amazing how simple things can calm a hurting body and head. You do what you've gotta do!

About the Author

Judith Briles, DBA, MBA

Dr. Judith Briles is CEO of The Briles Group, Inc., a Colorado-based research, speaking, training and consulting firm. She is internationally acclaimed as a keynote speaker and recognized as an expert in solutions to workplace issues. Her clients include hospitals and health care associations and organizations throughout North America. In 2002, her company was selected as one of the Top 100 Women Owned Businesses in Colorado by *ColoradoBiz* magazine. She is the recipient of the Distinguished Woman Award from the Girl Scouts in 2004, and was featured in *Who's Who of American Women* and *Who's Who Among Executives and Professionals in Nursing and Healthcare*.

Judith is an award winning and best selling author of 24 books including *Zapping Conflict in the Health Care Workplace* (a main selection of the Nurse's Book Society), *The Confidence Factor* (winner of 2002 Best Business Book from the Colorado Independent Publishers Association), *Woman to Woman 2000* (*Chicago Tribune's* Business Book of the Year), *The Briles Report on Women in Healthcare* (featured selection of the Nurses' Book Club), *10 Smart Money Moves for Women* (winner of the 2001 Colorado Book Award for non-fiction), *Smart Money Moves for Kids* (winner of the 2001 Colorado Independent Publishers Association Award for Self-Improvement/Parenting), *The Dollars and Sense of Divorce, GenderTraps,* and *When God Says NO. Stabotage! How to Deal with the Pit Bulls, Skunks, Snakes,*

Scorpions & Slugs in the Health Care Workplace is her 25th book. Her books have been published in 16 countries.

Dr. Briles has been featured on over 1,000 radio and television programs nationwide and writes the "Career Moves" column for the *Denver Business Journal.* Her work has been featured in *The Wall Street Journal, Time, People, USA Today* and *The New York Times.* She's a frequent guest on *CNN* and is the resident money expert on Denver's *CW2.*

She is the founder of the Colorado Authors Hall of Fame and known as The Book Shepherd. Judith is president of the Colorado Authors League, serves on several advisory boards and is a past director of the National Speakers Association, the Woman's Bank of San Francisco, Colorado Women's Leadership Coalition, the Colorado Independent Publishers Association, and the Colorado Nurses League.

For information about Judith Briles' availability for speeches and to subscribe to her newsletter, contact her at:

JudithBriles@aol.com or **Judith@Briles.com**
www.Briles.com
www.TheBookShepherd.com

303-627-9179 ~ 303-627-9184 Fax
The Briles Group, Inc.
PO 460880
Aurora, CO 80046

Dr. Judith Briles

Creating Workplace and Personal Excellence

Keynotes, General Sessions and Workshops

Especially for Health Care Professionals!

Creating Confidence Out of Chaos

Based on the best-selling book, The *Confidence Factor-Cosmic Gooses Lay Golden Eggs,* attendees will learn that confidence is acquired, not inherited; and it usually comes from the pitfalls—the cosmic gooses—of life. Woven around the 10 Steps to Building Confidence, this stimulating and humorous speech is guaranteed to motivate and inspire audiences. With confidence, anything is possible. This keynote/general session has consistently received outstanding evaluations.

Stabotage!™ Dealing with the Pit Bulls, Skunks, Snakes, Scorpions & Slugs in the Workplace

Every workplace has them—the pit bulls that hide behind lipstick and designer clothes; skunks that look harmless yet create stinkfests; snakes who flick their abrasive tongue and voice at any and all; the scorpions who sting you with a slap of their heavy backhand; and the slugs ... those who are "just there" and breathing, barely. The effect is that huge amounts of money are lost in reduced productivity, turnover-related costs and patient safety factors. Staboteurs™ can be very visible or they can operate on a stealth basis. There are differences in how male and female staboteurs™ create chaos and who they are likely to target. When there are staboteurs™ in the midst, good and great employees declare their workplace is toxic—the pits—and leave.

Participating in this workshop which was based on a study completed in the fall of 2007 with more than 3,000 respondents, you will learn how to effectively deal with the bad girls and boys of the workplace. Included is Judith's revised CarefrontingScript™ Model, updates on the latest in communication techniques in dealing with conflicts and toxic behavior, plus tools and quizzes.

Dealing with WMDs and Pit Bulls in Your Workplace

Every workplace has its fill of Conflict Creators, Saboteurs in the Midst, and Red Ink Behaviorists who are waiting for the retirement bell (even if it's five years away). The effect is that huge amounts of money are lost in productivity, turnover-related costs and patient safety factors. Based on nine national studies released in *Zapping Conflict in the Health Care Workplace, The Briles Report on Women in Health Care, Woman to Woman: From Sabotage to Support* and the forthcoming book, *Stabotage!* Participants will practice role-playing in the CarefrontingScript™, and learn how to effectively deal with the bad boys and girls of the workplace.

What the Bleep Did You Say #%&!?

Are you communicating? With whom? You might think you are, but only your colleagues know for sure! Rarely is a communication style wrong, just different. Learn the four steps to effective communicating, both as a listener and speaker, and identify the key factors that impede successful communication. Learn how to avoid the pitfalls of sharing too much information and why listening is the key to resolving conflict and to successful negotiation.

Money $marts

The "average" person spends over 10,000 days making money. How many days are you willing to commit to keeping some of it ... and better yet, making it grow? Based on Judith Briles' book, *Money $marts: Personal Financial Success in 30 Days!*, participants will learn practical tips and take away an action plan to build a stronger financial future, no matter what happens to Social Security.

Theories are bypassed and realistic strategies are presented. This program gets to the point. Useful and practical concepts are identified that participants can immediately implement. The result— you will reduce debt, eliminate waste, and create a safety net and a realistic strategy that allows the participant to be financially independent and survive economic challenges. Money issues are huge for today's health care professional.

Want Book?

How would you like to write the book you've dreamed of, even become a best-selling author? Most people have a book in them. Will yours get birthed, or will it die because it never was never properly conceived? Books create credibility. Whether your dream is to write the great novel, a children's series or a book that will enhance your professional credibility, this fast-paced session is for you. The business of publishing will be revealed; you will learn how to create titles that soar, how to structure a book, how to get started, whether you should publish with a traditional publisher or self-publish, and much more.

You will learn from a master book shepherd. Judith Briles is the author of 25 books—many of them award-winning. She has sold in excess of 1,000,000 copies, sold multiple foreign rights to 16 countries, created her own publishing imprint, has been featured on more than 1000 TV and radio shows—from *Oprah* to *CNN*—and print media from the *Wall Street Journal* to the *National Enquirer*, columnist for several publications including the *Denver Business Journal*, sought-after speaker for conferences and associations, is the resident "money" expert on Denver's CW2 and is the first recipient of the Lifetime Achievement Award from the Colorado Independent Publishers Association.

Judith knows the publishing and speaking worlds. To many, she's known as Colorado's Book Shepherd. Her website is *TheBookShepherd.com* (her speaking website is *Briles.com*). Celebrate Nurses Week and Hospital Week with a New Approach ... Book the set of Mini Talks—perfect for any workplace where time is in short supply. Create a menu of vignettes ... a condensed version of a fuller program where employees can take an "extended" break of 30 up to 60 minutes. Choose the above programs as well as from Judith's website, www.Briles.com, under Programs.

To check availability, contact Judith's office at
800-594-0800
or email her at
Judith@Briles.com
or
JudithBriles@aol.com